GRACE

AT

30,000

FEET

AND OTHER UNEXPECTED PLACES

GRACE

AT

30,000

FEET

AND OTHER UNEXPECTED PLACES

KENT HANSEN

REVIEW AND HERALD® PUBLISHING ASSOCIATION
HAGERSTOWN, MD 21740

Unless otherwise indicated, all Scripture references are from the New Revised Standard
Version (NRSV) of the Bible, copyright © 1989 by the Division of Christian Education of
the National Council of the Churches of Christ in the U.S.A. Used by permission.

Texts credited to Message are from *The Message.* Copyright © 1993, 1994, 1995,
1996. Used by permission of NavPress Publishing Group.

Scripture quotations marked NASB are from the *New American Standard Bible,* copyright © 1960, 1962, 1963, 1968, 1971, 1972, 1973, 1975, 1977, 1994 by The Lockman
Foundation. Used by permission..

Texts credited to NEB are from *The New English Bible.* © The Delegates of the
Oxford University Press and the Syndics of the Cambridge University Press 1961, 1970.
Reprinted by permission.

Texts credited to NIV are from the *Holy Bible, New International Version.* Copyright
© 1973, 1978, 1984, International Bible Society. Used by permission of Zondervan
Bible Publishers.

Texts credited to NKJV are from the New King James Version. Copyright © 1979,
1980, 1982 by Thomas Nelson, Inc. Used by permission. All rights reserved.

Scripture quotations marked NLT are taken from the *Holy Bible,* New Living
Translation, copyright © 1996. Used by permission of Tyndale House Publishers, Inc.,
Wheaton, Illinois 60189. All rights reserved.

Bible texts credited to NRSV are from the New Revised Standard Version of the
Bible, copyright © 1989 by the Division of Christian Education of the National Council
of the Churches of Christ in the U.S.A. Used by permission.

Texts credited to REB are from *The Revised English Bible.* Copyright © Oxford University Press and Cambridge University Press, 1989. Reprinted by permission.

This book was
Edited by Larry Becker
Copyedited by Jocelyn Fay and James Cavil
Designed by Tina Ivany
Front cover photo by PhotoDisc
Typeset: Bembo 11/14

PRINTED IN U.S.A.

06 05 04 03 02   5 4 3 2 1

R&H Cataloging Service
Hansen, Kent
    Grace at 30,000 feet and other unexpected places.

    1. Religious life.   2. Spiritual life.   I. Title.
                248

ISBN 0-8280-1697-6

This book is dedicated to

my father, Ted Hansen, who told me great stories;
my mother, Lois Hansen, who taught me to write them down;
my beloved, Patricia, who encourages me to write the truth; and
my son, Andrew, whose life and love is a continuing source of inspiration.

Thank you all for your belief in the best of me.

Acknowledgments

This book exists because of the care and effort of many people, some of whom I wish to acknowledge here for their direct contributions.

Jon McTaggart is a true companion in my search for the God of all grace. He was the first person who suggested that I turn my e-mail messages into a book. His advice on publication was invaluable. I am guided by his uncompromising zeal for Christ and his Midwestern common sense.

Terry Acosta is my excellent legal secretary and friend of eight years. This book has been a labor of love for her to the point that she developed wrist pain in correcting my "hard returns" in the original text. My son, Andrew, who spent a good portion of his summer vacation in helping prepare the manuscript, assisted her in the effort. I am grateful for their help.

Writing out of one's own life experience is a necessary but dangerous thing to do. My friends Jane Vickers, Patti Cotton Pettis, and Vicky Polan and my wife, Patricia, served as clear-eyed reality checkers to ensure that my expressions of grace are truthful and my statements of truth are gracious. If I have missed the mark it is in spite of them, not because of them.

The late *V. Norskov Olsen,* theologian and Loma Linda University president, spent many hours discussing with me the ideas that inform my writing. He opened my eyes to dimensions of the freedom and equality of men and women in Christ that I hope are accurately described in this book as a testament to my teacher.

Richard Osborne, the president of Pacific Union College, is a wellspring of thoughtful comments to me about life and writing. His distribution of my stories and essays were an essential connection in the publication of this book.

Roy Mann, my law partner, mentor, and personal attorney, has disciplined both my thinking and writing by rigorous insistence on clear use of language and intellectual honesty.

My brother, *Terry Hansen,* led me to the writers Gordon MacDonald and Brennan Manning, who in turn brought me to a spiritual sunrise of grace.

Joyce Smith is a sister of my heart and faithful hiking companion with whom many of these stories were first shared and who taught me the transforming power of forgiveness.

Warren Johns and *Bob Nixon* are two attorneys and friends who have long supported my message of God's grace to our colleagues in the legal profession by giving it a forum in the pages of *JD* magazine. Warren insisted for a decade that I had a book to write. I hope he is pleased.

Larry Becker, editor of *Vibrant Life* magazine, "discovered" my writing and brought it to the attention of the good folks at the Review and Herald Publishing Association. His skill as an editor and his friendship to me since our college days enabled the creation of this book out of a disparate collection of stories and musings. He shares my desire that everyone have the opportunity to become personally acquainted with Christ. It is our prayer that this book will stir an irresistible longing for that meeting in its readers.

The Review and Herald Publishing editorial staff members are a blessing of kindness and competence to a first-time author. They believed in this book before I did. May their support be rewarded by the spread of the gospel of grace.

Under the mercy of Christ,

Kent Hansen
Corona, California
December 2001

Contents

Introduction

God became one of us in Jesus Christ. This means that His presence is found in the ordinary places of our existence—our work, our leisure, our families, and our friendships.

There is a tendency to relegate our relationship with God to a once-a-week visit to His house, if we think about it at all. Much of our disappointment with the religious life is that it seems so impractical and irrelevant to the demands of our everyday living.

Coming to the knowledge that God loves us as we are opens the door to His presence with us 24 hours a day, seven days a week. While the Scripture is clear that we are saved by God's grace, it contains many more references to grace as the power by which we live a life pleasing to God and enjoyable to us as His children.

Why do we need this grace? Look around you. Technology and excellent methods of communication network our world. Yet so many of us are afflicted by stress, lacking in meaningful relationships, and scrambling for emotional survival amid material prosperity. We are anxious for personal security, but we feel a vague, pressurized dread that we are inadequate for the demands of our circumstances.

As a lawyer, I witness conflict and alienation every day between corporations, institutions, and individuals. It is right in the midst of those problems that I discovered God's transforming power to change lives through love and forgiveness, first in my life and then moving on to others who share their hopes and struggles with me. That power is not held in some legal formula or self-improvement program. It is found in the willingness of Christ to touch us and hold us in our joys and our most desperate moments and biggest messes.

Several years ago I began to send weekly e-mail letters to six friends, telling them that God cared about them as they started their workweek. My objective was to communicate an honest, positive, realistic description of God's love to hardworking men and women in the midst of the stressful marketplace. These six friends passed on the messages, and the number of persons requesting to receive them grew to hundreds. Clearly there is a hunger in many to know a God who is interested and involved in their lives.

The purpose of this book is the same as those messages—to describe a God who, through Jesus Christ, relentlessly pursues a relationship with men and women in the places where they fall in love, make deals, raise their children, earn their living, experience pain and loss, build friendships, face temptation and fall, and endure loneliness and broken hearts. In other words, I tell stories of a real God for real men and women.

The Gospel of John tells us that when Jesus took on human flesh and moved into our neighborhood He brought grace and truth with Him as gifts from the Father's heart (John 1:14, 17, 18). I seek to continue in Jesus' path by telling true stories about grace. I hope that in reading them you will be encouraged to want to get to know Jesus and the Father better and trust Them with every part of your life.

ONE

Grace at 30,000 Feet

*A stressed-out, backslidden attorney has a "road to Damascus"
experience while flying home from a business trip.*

I am a lawyer. Lawyers like questions. In fact, in law school they teach us that the questions are more important than the answers.

Jesus asked the best question I know. One day in the last week of His life He was interrogated by the chief priests, scribes, Pharisees, and Sadducees who were seeking to trip Him up and destroy His authority.

Jesus tired of the game. He asked the Pharisees a question: "What do you think of the Christ? Who is he?" No one was able to give Him an answer, nor from that day did anyone dare to ask Him any more questions (Matthew 22:41, 46).

"What do you think about Jesus Christ?" is the ultimate question. Pat answers won't suffice. What our parents, grandparents, spouse, or friends think won't cut it. No one can stand in for you or me in answering the ultimate question, because either Jesus Christ is our personal Savior and Lord or He is nothing to us.

Jesus said that doing good deeds—even as excellent as preaching the gospel, prophesying, and exorcising demons—won't save us. The answer to the ultimate question and the key to the kingdom of God is found, He said, in personal relationship with Jesus Christ (Matthew 7:21-23; John 17:3). I know this to be true.

I grew up in a Christian home, went to Christian schools, married a Christian spouse. My efforts were rewarded with scholarships, awards, and a good job.

In 1989 I was a busy young attorney on the rise—managing partner of my law firm, civic leader, father of a precocious 2-year-old son, and restoring an old home with my spouse. This is the stuff of the American dream.

But there was a sinkhole underneath. For one thing, I was totally consumed with work, oblivious to everything else. For another, I was spiritually bankrupt. I represented a Christian denomination and its flagship university, my alma mater. But the institution was in a civil war over its future, and as its legal counsel I was right in the middle. Religion was a business to me, and it was bad business.

There were warning signs of problems. Flare-ups of anger. Tears of unnamed sadness while driving from appointment to appointment.

I needed to travel to the church's headquarters for a meeting. On the way out the door leaving home, I picked up a book to read on the plane. My first choice was a novel. Something in me said no. The next book in the pile was a book my brother had told me about—*Ordering Your Private World,* by Gordon MacDonald. (Oliver-Nelson, 1985). Thinking it was a time-management book, I'd ordered it through a secular bookstore in town. Settling on the plane, I was surprised to find it was a Christian book.

MacDonald's premise is that each of us has an inner world of the heart and soul where our self-esteem is formed and basic decisions about motives, values, and commitments are made. This is the interior space where we commune with God. It has five sectors—motivation, time, intellectual growth, spirit, and Sabbath peace. If these interior sectors are properly centered in Christ and exercised by spiritual and intellectual disciplines, our outer world of relationships will also be healthy. If this inner world is not ordered, we can disintegrate in stress and dysfunction.

MacDonald contrasts the drivenness of King Saul of Israel with the calling of John the Baptist. Drivenness can trap us in a high-maintenance golden cage of success, leaving us spiritually drained, leading to a disastrous spiritual and moral collapse. It wasn't many pages before I thought, *He's talking about me.* I read on with a mixture of curiosity and dread.

When I reached the hotel in Maryland, I watched the end of the baseball playoffs out on the West Coast, then read some more. Continuing my reading the next morning, I thought, *I should pray.* But there was a problem. Lifelong professed Christian that I was, graduate of Christian schools, son of praying Christian parents—I couldn't pray. I mean, what do you say to God when you aren't trying to pass a test, win a case, or make a deal? I paced the room in growing frustration. I couldn't pray. Finally I blurted out something incoherent to this effect: "God, I'd like to talk to You, but I don't know how."

The day was filled with business, but not resolution to the institutional conflict. The next morning went the same way with my reading and struggle to pray. My flight home included a change of planes in Chicago. At 1:00 p.m., just after takeoff from O'Hare International Airport, I read this prayer that MacDonald quoted from an old Salvation Army evangelist, Samuel Logan Brengle:

"Keep me, O Lord, from waxing mentally and spiritually dull and stupid. Help me to keep the physical, mental, and spiritual fibre of the athlete, of the man who denies himself daily and takes up his cross and follows Thee. Give me good success in my work, but hide pride from me. Save me from the self-complacency that so frequently accompanies success and prosperity. Save me from the spirit of sloth, of self-indulgence, as physical infirmities and decay creep upon me" (p. 151).

I was in the window seat. The plane was still on its ascent. As I read this prayer I heard a distinct audible voice, and God said to me: "You are convicted of sin. Your pride and busyness have choked Me out of your life and are killing your relationship with your family. Don't you think I can take care of the university and everything else you're concerned about? Trust Me."

That was it. It affected me physically. I squirmed in my seat, heart racing. For months afterward I felt tender and raw, like I had been burned out inside. Setting the book aside, I stared out the window, stunned. This was real and overpowering. All I could do was yield to the presence of a God who had just run me over with the big Mack truck of grace.

When we landed in Ontario, I knew I had to tell my wife, Patricia, what had happened. When I pulled into the driveway, she came out to meet me. "We need to go pick up Andrew at the baby-sitter," she said.

"OK. But first I have to tell you something."

"Is everything OK?" she asked.

"Well, yes and no."

We sat down in the living room. I told her what had happened. Then I said, "Every bit of talent that God has given me for leadership and organization I have squandered. I do all these things and then, as if that weren't enough, I start new organizations. I don't ask God if I should do any of these things.

"I come home late and eat supper and play with Andrew awhile. Then I go upstairs and shut the door and work past midnight, night after night. No one else in the firm does that. I do it just to show I can do all this stuff and more. I come in after you are asleep, and I'm up and out before you're awake.

"You're ill and are fighting the loss of your eyesight. When you're angry and upset about it, I just dismiss you by saying, 'Don't dump this on me.'"

I looked at her and said, "I have been so selfish, and I am sorry, so sorry that I am sick in my bones. Things are going to have to be different. It would help if you were in this with me."

Patricia looked at me awhile, then said, "Things have been out of control for a long time. We have gone from a great marriage to an ordinary marriage. I want this too."

We bowed our heads and prayed together. Then we went and picked up our son.

The differences were immediate and lasting. I developed an enormous appetite for God's Word. God left nothing in our lives unturned. From three active believers in my office at the time, 15 people since then have accepted Christ or renewed a relationship with Him. It all happened quietly without proselytizing. Prayer, encouragement, and the witness of a changed life have power. I quit eight board and committee memberships in a day. My life became centered in Christ and the quiet time I spend in study and prayer with Him every morning.

God didn't change my life in a pew or a classroom. He changed it in the real world where I love my wife, play with my son, make deals, argue cases, and write contracts. I will tell you now after the devastation of grace that I am more sure of God than ever, and less sure of everything else. At every turn in the road God has become much greater and more encompassing than I thought before. Everything else continues to fade. I begged Him for a while to leave some things alone, but He is relentless in His changing grace. I could never go back.

You may be longing to take the same path but struggling to know how to proceed. Why not try telling God what I told Him in that hotel room: "God, I want to talk to You, but I don't know how"?

If you ask, I think you'll receive the answer to the ultimate question.

TWO

Night Watch

A young lawyer/father discovers the loving presence of God while holding his infant son against his chest during night feedings.

Patricia is asleep. Andrew is crying. I'm awake. This is natural selection. So I take a bottle from the refrigerator door and put it in the warmer. Andrew expects more than me when I pick him up. He screams when he doesn't get it right away.

"It's OK. I've got him," I call in to a stirring Patricia.

The details are hazy: grab the bottle with one hand and test its warmth by dribbling some milk on the other wrist—too hot. Fumble to turn the faucet on; run cool water over the bottle. Another wrist splash. (I don't feel anything) and on into his mouth.

Andrew's face at these moments is screwed up to make a fitted coupling for the nipple. The connection is everything, and his sucking noises say, "It's a go!"

Back in his room, I turn off the light and sit in the rocker. Three a.m. I'll be in court in five and a half hours. What about the contract due tomorrow afternoon? I have a million racing thoughts in the dark. I'm confused and disoriented. I cannot serve both God and mammon, be in two places at once. I cannot be both father and lawyer on a Monday at 3:00 a.m.

Andrew turns in toward my chest and wriggles down in my arms. He is a round bundle to my dark-adjusted eyes. He is my boy. He depends on me.

My consciousness focuses on him. His little ear and cheek are pressed against my naked chest. It is very dark. Life here and now amounts to three things—supporting arms, warm milk, and a steady heartbeat.

In this very moment I know that I am loved even as I love. "Can a woman forget her nursing child, and not have compassion on the son of her womb? Surely they may forget, yet I will not forget you" (Isaiah 49:15, NKJV).

Thank You, dear Father, for the very idea of communion. From Your heart to mine, from mine to his—a living love. Amen.

THREE

Sunflower Gospel

Father and son discover the grace of God revealed in growing things, answered prayers, and the gracious healing of a broken sunflower stalk.

My son, Andrew, and I planted a garden together when he was 5. He is growing up in a Southern California city, unlike my rural upbringing in the hills of coastal central California.

Wanting to teach Andrew the secrets of growing things, his grandpa and I built a 2' x 4' x 8' box. I filled it with $70 worth of compost, soil amendment, topsoil, sand, and steer manure—a suburban lawyer's and Home Depot's idea of "bottomland."

Andrew poked tiny holes with a stick, making ragged rows for lots and lots of carrots and radishes. We also planted lettuce, beets, and cabbage. He made a face at the thought of eating them. "You don't need to eat it to grow it," I told him.

The final row was devoted to heart-shaped sunflower seeds. I stuck my index finger up to the first knuckle in the soft dirt. Andrew carefully dropped in the seeds. His hands patted little mounds over them.

Two nights later I drove Andrew to the store. "Dad," he said, "we forgot rain for our garden."

"I watered it, son."

"We need rain for our garden."

"Do you want to ask Jesus for rain?"

He nodded.

"OK, you ask Him first, and then I'll pray."

I could see his hands folded and his eyes glued shut in the light of the passing freeway signs.

"Dear Jesus, we need rain for our garden so that it will grow vegetables. Please send us some. I love You, Jesus. Amen."

"Dear Jesus . . ." I began.

"Dad! Don't close *your* eyes; you're driving," Andrew interrupted.

Two nights later it rained through the night unexpectedly. Southern California endured a long drought between 1990 and 1992. But this was a gentle rain, the first in a long time. Though it was gone by morning, it was just enough to soak the new seeds.

I showed Andrew the wet street out the window when he woke up. "Do you remember that you asked Jesus for rain? He sent it."

"Of course," he said.

Several days later it began to rain again. The drought broke. It poured almost every day for more than a month.

On the way home from preschool one afternoon Andrew asked his mom if he could ride his new bike when he got home.

"Not today, sweetheart. It's raining."

"Mom," he said thoughtfully, "do you remember when I asked Jesus for rain for my garden?"

"Yes."

"I think He thought I meant forever."

When the plants grew up, we thinned them out. The sunflowers needed more room, so we took out all but two plants.

Someone stomped through our garden one afternoon. A small footprint smashed a row of carrots. A gum wrapper was tossed between rows. One of our two sunflower plants was snapped. It was about three feet high, beginning to bud. The stalk was broken in the middle. Some of its fibers were shredded. The top half hung limp over the side of the garden box.

Andrew was upset. So was I, even more. We argued about who could have done this thing. I thought maybe a kid.

"No," he declared. "A kid would never do something like that! A grown-up would."

The anger and sadness turned to suspicion. "Did you do this?" I asked him.

Andrew was indignant. Lifting one foot up until I could see the sole of his shoe, he demanded, "Do you see this foot?"

"Yes."

He pointed at the footprint in the garden. "Do you see that footprint?"

"Yes." The footprint was obviously bigger than his foot.

"Do you think this foot made that print?"

"No." I averted my eyes and mumbled, "I'm sorry." The son of a lawyer had learned his lessons well. The defense rested, having destroyed the prosecution's case. Andrew huffed off across the yard.

I reached down to pull out the plant, but I couldn't do it. We had placed the seed in the ground and watched it grow. We had thinned out the other plants, choosing this one to grow. We had watered it and protected it.

Now I could not kill it. I would wait until it turned brown and withered before I pulled it out. *Silly,* I thought, *but I can't destroy what I love.*

A week later I noticed a surprising thing. The plant still hung down, but its head twisted around so its bud faced the sun. The stalk was contorted. It looked unnatural, even painful.

The broken plant continued to rise as the days passed. It reached the point where it stood straight out at a 45-degree angle from the broken place. The torn fibers strained but held. The bud turned into a blossom, and the warm sun drew its namesake up toward it. I marveled.

The weight of the blossom appeared too much for the broken stalk to bear. There was nothing going for the plant but life itself.

The stalk straightened and thickened at the torn place. It actually became stronger there.

We went on vacation for 10 days. I raced to see the sunflower when we came home. The sunflower bloomed full—a dark chocolate face surrounded by yellow petals. It was taller than its companion plant.

The head became so heavy with seeds that I thought the stalk would break again. It held, but leaned far out of the box. The seeds filled at its heart in an intricate concave pattern. Bees fed on the sweetness of the big flower.

Andrew brought friends and visitors to look at the huge flower. They were quiet when I told them the story of the broken plant that I couldn't bear to destroy.

The disciple Andrew brought some curious visitors to see the full flower of God's love one afternoon. Jesus used the occasion to explain the facts of life in the kingdom. "The hour has come for the Son of Man to be glorified. I tell you the truth, unless a kernel of wheat falls to the ground and dies, it remains only a single seed. But if it dies, it produces many seeds. . . . Now my heart is troubled, and what shall I say? 'Father, save me from this hour'? No, it was for this very reason I came to this hour. . . . But I, when I am lifted up from the earth, will draw all men to myself" (John 12:23-32, NIV).

My Andrew had not read these words yet. But he saw the sunflower, and he knew what it meant.

I had read these words many times, but I never knew their meaning until I saw the sunflower. A hard heart-shaped seed dies to live. Wounds become points of strength. The greatest glory springs from brokenness. That glory belongs to the Father and Son, who, in Their love, cannot bear to destroy what They have planted and watered.

It's true for you and me, you know. Jesus will not break a bruised reed or snuff out a smoldering wick (Matthew 12:20).

This is the sunflower gospel. This is the truth of grace.

FOUR

The Frame Without a Picture

A life without Christ, no matter how good-looking,
is a frame without a picture.

One late summer afternoon I appeared in the office of the chief executive of a large Christian service organization. I was there to report on my investigation of a sexual harassment incident involving two employees. The conduct was so egregious and callous that the woman complainant was hospitalized for an emotional breakdown. I concluded my report with a question: "How could a thing like this happen here?"

The CEO stood and walked to the office window. Sunlight, screened through elm trees, dappled the conference table between us. With a sigh the answer came. "Jesus has a hard time working here. We are very broken people, but we don't admit it. So Jesus has a hard time working here, because Jesus only works in brokenness."

There was silence for a moment, and then the CEO continued: "We have a beautiful picture frame here. Grounds, buildings, and a mission statement. But we miss the picture because we don't acknowledge the hole in the middle of the frame. That's why things like this happen."

Then this powerful, celebrated executive told me a surprising thing. "I have a beautiful frame on the wall at home with no picture in the middle. A portrait of Jesus is supposed to be placed in the frame. The empty frame reminds me every day that I need Jesus."

That was an achingly honest moment. For most of us the frame is our carefully put-together exterior—the smile, the competency, the bravado. The hole in the middle is the hole in our gut, the emptiness in our heart that lets us know that something or someone is missing. What do we seek to fill that hole in us? We all have different answers—people, food, alcohol, shopping, money, work, sex, religious activity.

When I was a child I would wander through the Woolworth's store in Santa Cruz waiting for my brother to finish his music lesson. One of the things that attracted my attention were the picture frames. There were all kinds of wood, glass, brass, and chrome frames. Each one of them contained a photograph of a really good-looking man or woman, a cute kid, an embracing family, or sometimes Marilyn Monroe or Elvis Presley. I would look at them and wonder, *Who are these people? Why is their picture on display? Why didn't their loved ones keep these pictures for themselves the way we keep our family pictures in frames at home?*

My mom told me that those people were models. The people who made the frames thought they would sell better if there was a picture of a handsome person in each one to attract curious shoppers.

This introduction to marketing left me unsatisfied. I knew the picture should be more important than the frame that held it. But these pictures were nothing more than smiles that said, "Buy me, hold me, take me home." There was no connection of story, no relationship, no love. We took photographs of the people that we knew and loved and put them on our walls and shelves at home just because of love. I could not understand why someone would buy a picture of someone they didn't know and didn't love just to get a frame. Something seemed terribly wrong about that to me.

No picture or a false picture—it makes no difference. No matter how beautiful the frame, there is a hole in the middle if there is no love and no story to go with the picture.

"One day one of the local officials asked Jesus, 'Good Teacher, what must I do to deserve eternal life?'

"Jesus said, 'Why are you calling me good? No one is good—only God. You know the commandments, don't you? No illicit sex, no killing, no stealing, no lying, honor your father and mother.'

"He said, 'I've kept them all for as long as I can remember.'

"When Jesus heard that, he said, 'Then there's only one thing left to do: Sell everything you own and give it away to the poor. You will have riches in heaven. Then come, follow me.'

"This was the last thing the official expected to hear. He was very rich and became terribly sad. He was holding on tight to a lot of things and not about to let them go.

"Seeing his reaction, Jesus said, 'Do you have any idea how difficult it is for people who have it all to enter God's kingdom? I'd say it's easier to thread a camel through a needle's eye than get a rich person into God's kingdom.'

" 'Then who has any chance at all?' the others asked.

" 'No chance at all,' Jesus said, 'if you think you can pull it off by yourself. Every chance in the world if you trust God to do it' " (Luke 18:18-27, Message).

Matthew refers to the fact that the official was young as well as rich (Matthew 19:22). He was the "rich young ruler." That was his carefully constructed frame to hold everything together. He was *rich*. He was *young*. He was *religious*. He was *in control—a ruler*. As Luke noted, the official was holding on tightly to a lot of things. That's what a frame does for us; it holds things together. But what if our frame holds together, but holds nothing? What do you do about the hole in the middle, the empty space, the hunger that just won't quit? Do you just smile a celebrity-quality smile and appear as a well-put-together package?

Jesus looked at the well-put-together package in front of Him. He listened to the young man's profession of zealous commandment keeping. Jesus knew that what He was looking at didn't add up.

"Jesus looked him hard in the eye—and loved him! He said, 'There's one thing left: Go sell whatever you own and give it to the poor. All your wealth will then be heavenly wealth. And come follow me' " (Mark 10:21, Message). Standard versions quote Jesus as telling the young man "You lack one thing" (see, e.g., NRSV). My attorney colleagues and I refer to slick corporate types as "empty suits." This refers to a polished appearance with a rather superficial, mechanical substance that lacks depth of belief or insight. The rich young ruler was an empty suit. Take away the packaging of wealth, youthful appearance, power, and piety, and what was left? Only a pleading question rising out of the gnawing emptiness inside: "What must I do to get eternal life?" The question spills the secret that the beautiful frame is missing its picture.

What does it mean to "lack one thing"? This exchange between Jesus and the young man confused the crowd, because some of them blurted out, "If being good and successful won't save us, who can be saved?" (see verse 26). Jesus responded with the ultimate truth of our existence: "It is not possible for you to ever acquire enough goodness and stuff to live through eternity. Your only possibility for eternal life is God. You have all this stuff, good stuff, but you lack the one essential travel item, God, and God won't fit unless you make room by getting rid of the stuff. Or put another way, how can you hang the picture if the frame's too big to get through the door?"

The frame without the picture is pretense. The Armani suit without a soul is delusion. The beautiful grounds and well-equipped buildings without a reliance on the Holy Spirit for operating guidance are deception and blasphemy. The relationship you feel you can control, the reputation you have so carefully constructed and burnished, the influence you have so carefully accumulated, the one little thing you claim as your physical or emotional possession—these are all counterfeit currency unable to buy life. Jesus spoke of a man who said to himself: "'Soul, you have ample goods laid up for many years; relax, eat, drink, be merry.' But God said to him, 'You fool! This very night your life is being demanded of you. And the things you have prepared, whose will they be?'" (Luke 12:19, 20).

Think about this. What would being rich, youthful, powerful, and religious do for you? Would it be enough? You may be rich or youthful or powerful or religious. Is it enough? Don't make the mistake of thinking this story is only about material wealth. It's about whatever we think we must have to live. That we live and how we live is explicitly stated in Scripture to be gift, not earnings. "For by grace you have been saved through faith, and this is not your own doing; it is the gift of God—not the result of works, so that no one may boast. For we are what he has made us, created in Christ Jesus for good works, which God prepared beforehand to be our way of life" (Ephesians 2:8-10).

Augustine wrote that each of us is created with a God-shaped hole in our heart. The space in the middle of my executive friend's frame is meant for Jesus. The space in the middle of the existence that we call life was meant for Jesus. It's not a place to accumulate people and stuff. Jesus Christ is the essence, the whole picture, of Christianity. Everything else—the pews, the pulpit, family values, Bible, art, doctrine, friendships, programs, prayer and fasting, even our own painstakingly nurtured virtue and self-image—are either methods, window dressing, or the extra gifts of a considerate God. The beating heart of the gospel, however, is Christ's: "For from him and through him and to him are all things. To him be the glory forever. Amen" (Romans 11:36). John laid it out simply: "God gave us eternal life, and this life is in his Son. Whoever has the Son has life; whoever does not have the Son of God does not have life" (1 John 5:11).

Jesus said: "Anyone who intends to come with me has to let me lead. You're not in the driver's seat; *I* am. Don't run from suffering; embrace it. Follow me and I'll show you how. Self-help is no help at all. Self-sacrifice is the way, my way, to saving yourself, your true self. What good would it do to get everything you want and lose you, the real you? What could you ever trade your soul for?" (Mark 8:34–36, Message).

For what will you trade your soul? No one ever bid at auction on the painting of an old master because the frame was nice.

Does the frame of your life lack a picture in the middle, or is the picture a smiling model that you don't know and don't love? It may be that your frame is scratched and battered, but it's all you have, or it may be that it is 24-karat gold. The real "you" was made in the image of God by the God who was meant to be the picture in the frame that is your body and soul. Anything or anyone else in that frame is an impostor. You may know this, but have simply forgotten the truth of it. The key now is to confess the missing picture, the hole in the middle of your heart to a Christ who says: "My grace is sufficient for you, for my power is made perfect in weakness" (2 Corinthians 2:9, NIV).

"Dear Jesus: Please move into my heart. Fill the empty spaces. Be the only picture in the frame that I offer You. Fill me with Your Holy Spirit and displace my desire for any substitutes for You. Thank You for loving me as Your own. Amen."

FIVE

The Washing

*A physician whose career was destroyed in a legal proceeding
and the lawyer who destroyed it find forgiveness and
reconciliation in the ordinance of foot washing.*

The Gospel of John contains this remarkable story:

"It was just before the Passover Feast. Jesus knew that the time
had come for him to leave this world and go to the Father. Having loved
his own who were in the world, he now showed them the full extent of
his love.

"The evening meal was being served, and the devil had already
prompted Judas Iscariot, son of Simon, to betray Jesus. Jesus knew that the
Father had put all things under his power, and that he had come from God
and was returning to God; so he got up from the meal, took off his outer
clothing, and wrapped a towel around his waist. After that, he poured
water into a basin and began to wash his disciples' feet, drying them with
the towel that was wrapped around him.

"He came to Simon Peter, who said to him, 'Lord, are you going to
wash my feet?'

"Jesus replied, 'You do not realize now what I am doing, but later you
will understand.'

"'No,' said Peter, 'you shall never wash my feet.'

"Jesus answered, 'Unless I wash you, you have no part with me.'

"'Then, Lord,' Simon Peter replied, 'not just my feet, but my hands
and my head as well!'" (John 13:2-9, NIV).

Dr. Smith was a controversial physician in my town.

There was a time, years ago, when he refused to take measures to
allow his terminally ill patients to breathe or to resuscitate patients in heart

failure. He didn't follow the policies of the local hospital when he did this. He knew the policies, but he disagreed with them. The policies required tests, procedures, and medical opinions that took time and money. Dr. Smith thought that this prolonged the agony of his patients and their families, so he made his own decisions and carried them out without regard for the policies.

The hospital's medical staff objected. There was an investigation, and there were charges against Dr. Smith. He would be dismissed from the medical staff if the charges were found to be true.

Dr. Smith was a smart, experienced physician. The physicians challenging him were intelligent and well-intentioned. As is true of most organizational conflicts, the issue was over authority. The divisions were deep and the conflict severe.

The medical staff held hearings and voted to dismiss Dr. Smith. He appealed to the hospital board and lost. Newspapers featured the story, because the life-and-death issues were sensational. The controversy was discussed throughout the community.

Ultimately Dr. Smith sued the hospital to keep his privileges to admit and treat his patients there. The hospital hired me to defend its interests.

At trial I began my opening statement by clarifying the issues in harsh terms: "Your Honor, Dr. Smith wants to quibble about the hearing procedures. I am here to talk about him killing people."

In the end the court ruled against Dr. Smith. He was dismissed from the medical staff and the staff of another nearby hospital. His practice was limited to the patients he saw in his office and a local nursing home. The dispute was an angry, humiliating episode, disturbing to all concerned.

Years passed. I experienced spiritual renewal in Christ and joined the same church that Dr. Smith attended. Each week I saw him there in the back pew with his wife.

After some time I became the local head elder. From time to time the pastor and I discussed reconciliation with Dr. Smith. The pastor had served on the hospital board at the time of the dismissal. The physicians who led the medical staff investigation also attended the church. None of us talked to Dr. Smith, because we feared rejection.

Then came a Communion. This meant foot washing, what my denomination calls "the ordinance of humility." Foot washing is the great divide of our congregation's Communion service. Many members get up and leave at this point of the service, unwilling to join in what they think is an awkward and meaningless ritual. And so it was with me. I hadn't participated in foot washing in years.

This particular day my wife was occupied with our little son, so I thought, *Well, I'll go wash feet. After all, I'm head elder.* I walked down the hall to the room where the men were gathered to wash each others' feet. I saw Dr. Smith standing in the doorway as I approached. Through the entire lawsuit and the years that followed, he and I had never spoken one direct word to each other. Now there was no way to pass without speaking to him.

I said, "Good morning, Doc."

"Do you have anyone to serve you?" he asked me.

"No."

He motioned for me to sit down. He got a basin of water. I sat down and removed my shoes and socks. He knelt down before me and washed my feet and dried them. When he was through I obtained fresh water and knelt down and washed his feet.

It was a moment in which I experienced true reverence. Emotions swept through me. I felt awe and humility, brokenness and tenderness, and thankfulness for a God who could break down the walls and create love between me and this man.

After drying his feet, I sat down beside Dr. Smith. "This is amazing considering everything that has happened between us," I remarked.

"Well," he said, "I've watched you and I've seen how Christ has changed your life."

I replied, "It's blessed me that you're here worshiping week after week after all that you've gone through."

He patted my arm. "I made mistakes and there have been misunderstandings, but the same Jesus who changed you has sustained me these past five years."

Then I said, "I'm sorry for all the pain this has caused you and your family."

We hugged, and remained friends to the day he died. Often we prayed for each other.

What is possible with God? A physician and a lawyer—the professional equivalent of "cats and dogs"; the prosecuted and the prosecutor—a man whose livelihood was attacked and the attacker—washed each other's feet and embraced. If I am ever asked if I've seen a miracle, I will tell about this. Such a thing is possible, but only in Christ.

When I told my experience to the surgeon who had prosecuted Dr. Smith before the medical staff, he too reconciled with Dr. Smith and sponsored his readmission to the medical staff.

"When he had finished washing their feet, he put on his clothes and returned to his place. 'Do you understand what I have done for you?' he asked them. 'You call me "Teacher" and "Lord" and rightly so, for that is what I am. Now that I, your Lord and Teacher, have washed your feet, you also should wash one another's feet. I have set you an example that you should do as I have done for you. I tell you the truth, no servant is greater than his master, nor is a messenger greater than the one who sent him. Now that you know these things, you will be blessed if you do them'" (John 13:12-17, NIV).

SIX

Being Found by Your Father

*A lost child and a seeking Father are the
essentials of the gospel of grace.*

The deer were muscled velvet in the early-morning sun. The herd grazed through the cabin clearing on tiptoe. They eyed me with lifted heads every time I moved on the porch.

I wanted to pet them, but they trotted off as I approached. Their flicking white tails led me into the woods as fast as my 4-year-old legs could go.

In my entrancement there was no time for goodbyes for my parents or brother. There was only the beckoning of marvelous creatures to join them in the mysterious forest.

Then I was alone. The deer vanished, leaving me the sound of an occasional twig snap and the staccato bursts of the omnipresent Steller's Jays.

The air hung thick with the scent of bear clover and warming pitch. I looked up to see only a ring of treetops, the cedars, firs, and sugar pines that grow thick along the canyon of the South Fork of the Merced River in the Sierra canyon called Wawona.

The sunlight poured down in honey-amber tubes flecked with dust and insects. Somewhere the river whispered, or was it the wind in the trees whose sound I had yet to know?

I turned around, every direction looking wonderful but the same. Lost, for the very first time. This day in the summer of 1957 I learned several life truths:

- There is a vague line between wonder and terror.
- Being alone under sky with growing things allows me to see things that I would otherwise never see and see them clearly.
- My father can find me anywhere.

His tenor call carried over logs and ravines and between trunks and rocks in two-syllable legato. "Ke-ent. Ke-ent."

I answered in lung bursts. "Daddy. Daddy. I'm here, Daddy."

Suddenly there he was, striding out of the shadows into my lostness. He swept me up, held me close in flanneled arms, and told me, "I love you." There is no experience like being found by your daddy.

Nearly 40 years later, embattled in the defense of a high-stakes lawsuit, I again lost my way. First I wandered into a thicket of charges and countercharges, pleadings and motions and deadlines. Bewildered and exhausted, I headed for the woods to renew the life truths. I sought the line between wonder and terror. I desired the insights visible under sky amid growing things. I wanted to be found by my Father.

Before dawn I entered the mountains to seek, but there was no finding. Then, on the fourth day, I tried a new trail. I was off course from the beginning. I answered the invitation of the running stream and the green meadow. But soon the trail left the stream and straightened out through a treeless valley. The August sun was warmer than I expected. I spotted an old beaver dam and scrambled down to the riverbed to explore it. Its brushy sides were sharp and jagged. When my bootlace caught on a limb, I jerked around and down, cutting my legs badly. When I got back on the trail, the dust congealed the blood, but the pain was grit and fire.

I walked on under the sun to the end of the valley. My water bottles lightened. My sweat made white-bordered continents of salt on my shirt. I took a different trail into the woods to return. For the second time in my life I was lost.

The ridges and thick trees obscured familiar landmarks. The valley disappeared. I ate my lunch in a stand of black oak. When I tried to read and pray there, the uncertainty of my surroundings would not permit rest. I walked on and on.

My water was consumed. Sweat wicked away quickly in the high altitude. A little chill of dehydration spasmed here and there. I didn't have a clue where I was, but I stumbled on with aching feet and legs. The trail was reduced to half on a cliff side. Past that spot I inched, inhaling and exhaling the ancient prayer "Lord Jesus Christ, Son of the living God, have mercy on me a sinner" with every three trudging steps.

The path wound down into a gulch. There were tall red-barked incense cedars there, and a stream trickling down pooled steps in the late-summer heat. It was a shady, silent spot. I sat on a rock and heaved breaths.

It was hard to focus. I washed my dirty, bleeding legs in the stream. But with no destination in sight, I waited. My wait and my silence were my prayer. I had nothing left.

Sometime in that afternoon I heard my Abba call me. In response, my heart began to fill with a song. I stood and walked downstream, resting after each finished line of the praise rising in me. The song echoed and stirred in me until I gave it voice in the cedar-vaulted canyon. Here it is as we've been singing it in our small-group's worship:

> May our prayers be to You as incense.
> May our praise ascend to Your throne.
> Hear the cry of our heart, dear Abba,
> "Come and make us Your own."

> For we are Your children,
> The lambs of Your care.
> We know You love us;
> This truth dispels our despair.

> May our prayers be to You as incense.
> May our praise ascend to Your throne.
> Hear the cry of our heart, dear Abba,
> "Come and take us home."

© 1996 by Kent A. Hansen

Singing my song in response to the love of the Abba who can find me anywhere, I walked out of the shadows into the light of the trailhead. There still is no experience like being found by your Father.

SEVEN

The Gospel of Scars

Discovering while hiking that wildflowers grow best in torn and scarred earth and grace grows best out of a broken heart

Hiking across country, I encounter old roads scarring the protective crust of the earth. They are ugly wounds in the soil and do not heal easily. There are still tracks in the Great Plains and the deserts of the American West that date from the wagon trains of the mid-nineteenth century.

In the spring, though, a remarkable thing happens. These ruts fill with wildflowers—blue lupines, orange poppies, and yellow buttercups in my part of the country. The wounds break up the hard surface and allow new and beautiful life to break through. It is a promise of hope beyond pain, or re-birth beyond destruction. Emerson said that wildflowers are God's laughter.

David wandered the hills and deserts of Israel and noted this phenomenon. He prayed in gratitude to God: "You visit the earth and water it. You greatly enrich it; . . . You water its furrows abundantly, settling its ridges, softening it with showers, and blessing its growth. You crown the year with your bounty; *your wagon tracks overflow with richness"* (Psalm 65:9-11).

Our Creator identifies with our scars. By the furrows whipped cruelly into the flesh of Jesus' back, we are healed, because He took them Himself so they wouldn't be carved into us (Isaiah 53:4, 5). Our life in Him is the wildflowers in the ruts.

We do bear scars, though. Some may be self-inflicted. Others are from those who thought they could make up what they lacked from our flesh or emotions. Some are the consequence of living in a broken, jagged world in desperate need of renewal. The psalmist prays: "They have greatly oppressed me from my youth. . . . Plowmen have plowed my back and made their furrows long. But the Lord is righteous; he has cut me free from the cords of the wicked" (Psalm 129:1-4, NIV).

Our scars tell us something very important—that we live in spite of what has befallen us. That gives us hope. They testify to the truth of our unspeakable experiences that we would otherwise be tempted to deny, and that gives us faith. They teach us compassion to comfort others experiencing the same wounds, and that gives us love.

In truth, the life that grows out of our wounds is the very power of God. "The things [people] do in secret it would be shameful even to mention. But everything, when once the light has shown it up, is illumined, *and everything thus illumined is all light*" (Ephesians 5:12-14, NEB). Brennan Manning writes about this power:

"God not only forgives and forgets our shameful deeds, but even turns their darkness into light. All things work together for those who love God, 'even,' Augustine of Hippo added, 'our sins.'

"Christians who remain in hiding continue to live the lie. We deny the reality of our sin. In a futile attempt to erase our past, we deprive the community of our healing gift. If we conceal our wounds out of fear and shame, our inner darkness can neither be illuminated nor become a light for others. We cling to our bad feelings, beating ourselves with the past, when what we should do is let go. As Dietrich Bonhoeffer said, guilt is an idol. But when we dare to live as forgiven men and women, we join the wounded healers and draw closer to Jesus" (Brennan Manning, *Abba's Child* [Colorado Springs, Colo.: NavPress, 1996], pp. 24, 25).

Paul described the entire process from wound to glory:

"All praise to the God and Father of our Master, Jesus the Messiah! Father of all mercy! God of all healing counsel! He comes alongside us when we go through hard times, and before you know it, he brings us alongside someone else who is going through hard times so that we can be there for that person just as God was there for us. We have plenty of hard times that come from following the Messiah, but no more so than the good times of his healing comfort—we get a full measure of that, too" (2 Corinthians 1:3-5, Message).

May wildflowers burst through your scars.

EIGHT

Out of Right Field

An awkward, shamed eighth-grade boy finds redemption in a remarkable catch during a softball game.

Once you were not a people, but now you are God's people; once you had not received mercy, but now you have received mercy" (1 Peter 2:10).

Baseball season, a glorious time when "hope . . . springs eternal within the human breast. . . . For Casey, mighty Casey, was advancing to the bat" (Ernest Thayer).

The start of each baseball season reminds me of a moment of sheer grace that changed my life forever. It is a story from deepest right field.

Do you know about right field? That's the place where no one hits the ball. That's where you were banished if you were a klutzy kid without motor control but the teacher made them pick you anyway—just to be fair.

I was the prototype of that kid. My eyes were crossed. My feet were big. I was truly afraid of the ball.

This was too bad, because softball was the sport of choice at Samuel Eizenfelt Memorial Junior Academy, the pink-tinged block-walled fortress of religious virtue where I attended elementary school. It was there that my cringing awkwardness led my classmates to call me "Spazo" (for "spastic") and "Cordo" (for "uncoordinated"). So what if I could play the piano, read more books than any other kid in the County Public Library's summer reading contest three years in a row, and owned my very own pony. I was a certainty to drop the ball and lose the game.

It did not help that my older brother Terry, a player of renown, had attended the school before me. He could catch, throw, and hit with aplomb and set the standard for play of which I was the inglorious exception.

We would line up at recess or PE class to pick sides. The best players would be captains. They would pick their teams by calling out their choices, who would leave the line and walk over to stand beside the captain who had chosen them. Good players went first, mediocre players next, and then I would find myself standing alone, except for Paulie Swenson. Paulie had a congenital eye problem that allowed him to see well only in the dark and required him to squint in daylight. Paulie would actually be chosen before me.

There was an uncomfortable silence while both teams stared at me standing alone at the edge of the grass. Finally the teacher would clear his throat and one of the captains would mutter, "I'll take Kent, but you have to let us be the home team."

The next words I would hear were inevitable. "Kent, you take right field." I would trudge out to the graveled wasteland behind first base where I was exiled in the hope that no ball would be hit to me and maybe I'd daydream and forget to come in to bat.

The major factor in our softball games was Mr. Messerschmidt, our rather odd eighth-grade teacher. He was an intense young man who glared at us through horn-rimmed glasses, and bow ties bobbed off his Adam's apple. His most remarkable feature was his shocking references to human anatomy and sexual relations, which frequently broke through his monotone lectures. These always left us embarrassed and quiet and appalled for our parents, who were locked in a perpetual argument with the principal about his fitness for employment.

Looking back with the benefit of 32 years, I realize that Messerschmidt was complicated and lonely, and I feel sorry for him. But there was no getting around it then; Messerschmidt was a mean, sarcastic man. He would call us names and disparage our intelligence. When I would muff a ground ball in four-square, fall down chasing a fly ball, or strike out to the chant of "Cordo" or "Spazo," he would smirk and laugh. This was mild. His favorite targets were shy, awkward girls just coming into the full bloom of their puberty. These he would tease unmercifully about their looks and their clothes, forcing them to red-faced, tearful silence.

Our softball games provided the canvas for the full portrait of Mr. Messerschmidt as bully. It is no challenge for a 27-year-old man to drive a ball over the heads of 13-year-old boys and girls. That is exactly what he would do, game after game, at-bat after at-bat. Playing with children allowed him his fantasy to be Babe Ruth. Attempts to walk him were met with his withering rancor about the courage of the pitcher. It was better to give in and let him hit and watch him laugh around the bases while the left and center fielders would give chase to the rolling ball over our fence-less diamond.

Macho hitters always pull the ball. My one relief was that right-handed Messerschmidt's inflated sense of manhood wouldn't allow him to swing late and hit the ball to right field.

So it went day after day until . . .

Karen Sykes was a classmate who lived on the school grounds with her parents, who were the school janitors. We were all invited to her birthday party on Sunday afternoon. We played a softball game before the cake and ice cream were served.

Karen was my friend, and she did a wonderful thing. She asked me to be a captain for the first time ever. I envied the good players, and I picked them then. Mr. Messerschmidt always expected to be selected first. On principle, I did not take him. Surprised and irritated, he pursed his lips and smirked. The other captain called his name.

We were the home team because I had picked first. Heady with my captainship, I put myself in left field, another first. This was met with the ill-disguised dismay of my teammates. Messerschmidt, batting third, hit a two-run homer in the first inning over the head of our center fielder. We scrambled back. Our games always had high scores.

Then came the third inning and my destiny. Messerschmidt came to bat with one out and one on base. It may give you some measure of the man to know that he was wearing a white shirt and bow tie at a kid's birthday party on a Sunday afternoon.

He looked at me out in left field. I was playing as deep as I possibly could to avoid the humiliation of the ball being hit over my head. I tell you truthfully that I had never caught a fly ball in the outfield in a game, ever! Messerschmidt knew this. With no illusions I gamely popped my big brother's black glove a few times with my fist and crouched as if I knew what I was doing.

There are moments for each of us that live forever suspended in time. For me these include my first kiss, winning a talent program, notification of my first published short story, the shame of almost being expelled my junior year of high school, Patricia saying yes, making law review, passing the bar, and standing in the law firm lobby, saying "Come to Daddy," while watching my grinning 18-month-old son toddle to me. And there is this third inning with one on and one out.

On a 2-0 count, Messerschmidt swung, and the ball arced high in the sunny blue sky over the left field line. I began to run toward the spot where I guessed the ball would come down. There is a sound track for my memory: gravel crunches beneath my thudding feet; my teammates' shouted encouragement are like cries of wheeling sea gulls; the wind rushes past my ears; my breath compresses and whooshes out.

I closed my eyes and stretched out my glove hand as far as my hurtling body would allow. The ball fell into my glove and stuck. I pulled up and stopped in foul territory.

My teammates erupted into screams. They had witnessed a miracle. "Did you see that? Kent caught Messerschmidt's fly." It happened when my eyes were closed. Skill had nothing to do with it. But I felt great!

Mr. Messerschmidt stood halfway between home plate and first base still holding his bat. He hurled away the bat in disgust. He glared at me, then walked away from the field and sat on a picnic table. In another measure of the man, he did not come out to the field in the bottom of the inning. He quit playing and sat by himself the rest of the party. Karen's mom had to bring him his cake and talk him into eating it.

The possibilities unlocked for me by the catch seemed limitless. That night I slipped the glove under my pillow. I lay in the dark, grinning at the ceiling and reliving every microsecond. The belief began to grow in me that I might be able to do this again.

My classmates forgot about the catch, but I couldn't forget. I began to talk anyone that I could into playing "three flys up" with me before and after school and at recess. I chased fly balls until my legs ached. In the summer I wore out all the neighbor kids by playing for up to six hours a day.

The remembered grace of the miracle catch breathed life into my practice.

When my freshman year began, the tapes that played the humiliating "Spazo" and "Cordo" over and over in my head began to fade. When it came time to play, I quickly moved the few feet between the ignominy of right field and the glory of the wide-open spaces of center field. There I played as captain of the championship intramural fast-pitch softball teams my senior year at Monterey Bay Academy, where I finished high school, and my senior year on the La Sierra campus of Loma Linda University.

Now I'm a middle-aged church league softball player, and I'm back in right field. That's OK. The lasting benefit of the catch remains with me.

I learned the key to grace for desperate moments in the adult version of right field, with my enemies muttering things that sound a lot like "Spazo" and "Cordo": closed eyes and outstretched hands. Skill has nothing to do with it. David must have played right field. He wrote about an experience that sounds a lot like it:

"Hear my prayer, O Lord. . . . For the enemy has pursued me, crushing my life to the ground. . . . Therefore my spirit faints within me; my heart within me is appalled. I remember the days of old, I think about all your deeds, I meditate on the works of your hands. I stretch out my hands to you. . . . Save me, O Lord, from my enemies; I have fled to you for refuge" (Psalm 143:1-9).

If this story reaches you when you are in deep right field, I want you to catch it. Let it stir you, awaken you, to the possibility of grace.

NINE

The Bonus

A legal secretary's faithfulness leads to answered prayer.

The economic recession of 1992 was a depression in Southern California. The downturn of the defense industry at the end of the cold war and the collapse of the savings and loan industry stagnated business and raised unemployment.

My law firm entered the period with almost twice the number of attorneys it had at the end. A large part of our business involves representing developers in planning and zoning processes. Property values tumbled, financing for home building was unobtainable, and our work dropped off. There were almost no new business start-ups, so advice on corporations and partnerships was not required. The effect on our attorneys and staff was grim.

Personal pension plans were cashed out to cover house payments. Houses were sold. New purchases were deferred. Incomes fell, in some cases by as much as two thirds. The uncertainty was a palpable icy chill in each of us.

My firm traditionally gives our staff a bonus in December. As managing attorney I hand it out on the morning of the annual holiday party. As we approached that day the shareholders faced the fact that there was no money for bonuses. We had at least avoided laying off staff, but a bonus was out of the question.

My heart was heavy when I wrote a message in each Christmas card: "Thank you for your hard work and support this past year. Your skill and gracious spirit blesses us all. These are difficult times, and the firm has not done well. We regret that we are unable to give a bonus. We ask for your help in making next year a better one."

I laid a card on each secretarial chair before I left the evening before the party. The office was quiet the next morning. I knew that they were disappointed and concerned. The bonus was not disposable income. For many of our employees it represented the financial step-ladder out of the old year. It also meant our success and position in the local community built throughout our 82-year history was endangered. None of us doubted that.

The office manager and I prayed together about the situation. On December 30 she came to me and said, "We have a little extra money that has come in." I checked with the other shareholders. They were entitled to a distribution of any profits. Without hesitation each one said, "Give the staff a bonus."

I wrote out new notes explaining that some late collections had made it possible to pay a bonus. I put a check in each one that represented about half of the usual bonus. On the morning of December 31 I went through the building handing out the envelopes.

I walked back down the hall toward my office. Yvonne, a young secretary, called out to me, "Mr. Hansen," as I passed her cubicle.

"Yes?" I stepped over to her desk.

Her blue eyes glistened. "Thank you for the bonus, Mr. Hansen."

"You're welcome."

"I have something that I want to tell you. This bonus is an answer to prayer."

"There were a lot of prayers," I said.

"I know, but God used this bonus to teach me to trust Him."

"How so?" I asked.

"The week after Thanksgiving our pastor told us about a special need in our church. I was moved to give, but the amount I was impressed to give was so large that I asked my husband about it. He said, 'That's a lot, but if you believe it's what God is telling you to do, let's go ahead.' So we gave.

"You know it's my first year here. The other secretaries told me that I would get a bonus on the day of the holiday party, so I wasn't worried. Then the day came and I got your card with no bonus. But I prayed, 'OK, God, take care of me.' We paid the house payment and the car payment and our other bills, and there was nothing left over. By the start of this week, I was wondering how we were going to make it. 'God,' I told Him, 'I know that You promised to be faithful to us. I don't know how this is going to work out, but I know You do. Thank You.'

"Then this morning you came by, and when I opened the envelope and saw the check I was overwhelmed. The amount on the check covers what we gave the church plus $50, to the penny. I just wanted you to know this and tell you thank you, Mr. Hansen. God is so good."

A managing attorney is not immune from glistening eyes. "Thank you, Yvonne, for telling me. Thank you more than you know. God *is* good. You've blessed me."

I walked back to my office, shut the door, and said thanks to the God of all grace, who is kind and faithful. Nineteen ninety-two was over, and 1993 was on its way. Time ahead is always a gift. We have known better days since then.

Time will be on all our minds this week—the past, never to be re-covered; the future, unknown. God's faithful grace covers all. Let us join with David in praying:

> But I trust in you, O Lord;
> I say, "You are my God."
> My times are in your hands (Psalm 31:14, 15, NIV).

TEN

Learning to Breathe

During a silent retreat a busy lawyer
rediscovers the simple blessing of breathing.

Several years ago, toward the end of a guided silent retreat, I awoke in the night to a profound change. Something was different, truly different in me, but what? Christ worked through the silent time of prayer and contemplation to bring me to a deeper heart knowledge of His love and grace for me. I was stripped down to the essence of my being. But now in the darkness, with the predawn sea breeze stirring my window's curtains and the killdeers piping as they ran through the fields outside, there was something new and good in me. But what? Lying there, I came to realize that it was a great and simple thing. I was breathing—great, deep, relaxed draughts of air. I was breathing in peace. I was breathing with the lungs of God.

I had forgotten how to breathe. Somewhere in my business, the conflicts of law that consume my days, the need to produce and to control, I forgot how to really breathe, just as I forgot how to trust. How do we forget things like that? We "grow up."

"There is a story making the rounds right now about a four-year-old girl who was overheard whispering into her newborn baby brother's ear. 'Baby,' she whispers, 'tell me what God sounds like. I am starting to forget'" (Robert Benson, *Between the Dreaming and the Coming True* [New York: Putnam Publishing Group, 2000], p. 55).

Jesus calls us back to remembrance: "Truly I tell you, unless you change and become like children, you will never enter the kingdom of heaven" (Matthew 18:3). In my childhood I would lie in the dark and consider the wonder of my beating heart and my breathing. Here I was again, 35 years later, remembering to breathe, enjoying the mystery of my life. I looked to the sheltering presence of my Abba that I knew was really there in the darkness, and I said, "Thank You."

Jesus encountered a Samaritan woman at Jacob's well in the town of Sychar. The woman was a seething mass of human need, dissatisfaction, religious prejudice, racial bias, and social alienation. In a phrase, "She was one of us."

Her condition was the human condition.

Jesus discerned that she believed she had to have a man to have a life— five prior marriages and a current live-in relationship. He used her need for water in the heat of the day to lead her to understand her real thirst—for a relationship with God, who loved and accepted her without condition of person, place, or thing. When she went back to town to tell her neighbors what she had learned, "the woman left her water jar" (John 4:28). She didn't need to conserve water when she possessed the spring. Her whole life changed that day. How great was that change? Does life in God change our need for basic things such as water, food, even breathing?

There was a deeper transaction in the story than the fulfillment of her need. It was the recognition that "God is spirit, and those who worship him must worship in spirit and truth" (verse 24). The word "spirit" here in the Greek is *pneuma*. It literally encompasses "breath," the rational soul, mental disposition, life, and mind—the basic ingredients of cognitive, sapient life itself. God's breath must be her breath. Her breath must be breathed by and for God. It is that basic. The Greek word for "worship" used in John's account *(proskuneo)* means a relationship so obeisant and reverential that the worshiper is like a dog licking its master's hand in love and gratitude. It means a flat-out, prostrate focus on the object of worship. When she took a breath or a drink of water after that I think she did it in the real context of a thankful, worshipful life. This breath-for-breath, dependent, focused worship of God became the core truth of her life. Must it become the core truth of ours?

Yes, God does not dress up our old life, improve our morals, eliminate our bad habits, and then monitor us for compliance. We'd die holding our breath if that were the case. God gives us a completely new life, eternal life in grace, and maintains that life in grace. The life God has to give us is His life. We live in God the life of God, and that relationship is so intimate that we are dependent on God for the very breath we breathe. We cannot receive a change more radical than a new life. I wonder if we really appreciate this fact.

"Blessed are the poor in spirit," said Jesus, "for theirs is the kingdom of heaven" (Matthew 5:3). The word "blessed" originates from a word for "fortunate" and "happy." The word "spirit" is again *pneuma,* the breath of life itself. The word "poor" *(ptochos)* is translated from a Greek word meaning an absolutely penniless beggar. The inheritance of the kingdom, the treasure found in our dying and resurrection with Christ, means that we accept our dependence on God for our very breath, for our life at its most elemental—air, water and bread. Eugene Peterson paraphrases Matthew 5:3 in *The Message* as follows: "You're blessed when you're at the end of your rope. With less of you there is more of God and his rule."

Jesus, dying as a human on the cross, lived out this truth to its conclusion. He cried out " 'Father, into your hands I commend my spirit.' Having said this, he breathed his last" (Luke 23:46). However, that wasn't the last breath He took on earth. After His resurrection He breathed on the disciples and said: 'Receive the Holy Spirit' " (John 20:22). So it is with us who believe. Paul told the Athenians:

"The God who made the world and everything in it, he who is Lord of heaven and earth, does not live in shrines made by human hands, nor is he served by human hands, as though he needed anything, since he himself gives to all mortals life and breath and all things. . . . For 'In him we live and move and have our being'; as even some of your own poets have said, 'For we too are his offspring' " (Acts 17:24-28).

It is our inheritance in Christ to live as children of God, breathing the fresh air of His grace. Have you forgotten this? This is a reminder of the deepest truth of your life: In God you live and move and have your very being, even the breath you are breathing this moment. Breathe in His peace.

ELEVEN

You Gotta Love Your Boy

A grieving father learns the story of the prodigal son from a homeless man on a sidewalk outside of an AA meeting.

Patricia, my beloved, used to help with children's ministries at our church. One day I heard her tell the other teachers, "Our one focus here is to teach these kids that God loves them because that's what stands between them and becoming really messed-up adults."

Do you know this love? Your head may tell you that it is theologically true, but do you hold this truth deep in your heart as the essential fact of your life? What a difference it makes for us to know that we are loved absolutely—no 'ifs,' 'ands,' or 'buts.' We can do basic things like breathe and laugh and love and tell the truth if we know that we are loved. It has to start somewhere, and in fact there is only one source. "In this is love," wrote John the Beloved, not that we loved God but that he loved us" (1 John 4:10).

A true story:

My friend John walked into an AA meeting one weekday morning about a block from my office in Corona. John is a successful business executive and it has been 27 years since he took his last drink. But he never forgets where he is coming from, what it cost him, and the grace that brought him through.

This particular morning he gathered with the motley assembly of men and women, young and old, affluent and poor, who comprise this AA group. John's heart was heavy with concern for his son, who was himself descending rapidly into a self-destructive spiral of alcohol abuse, rage, and violence. The boy was in jail at that moment after a terrifying binge of drinking, theft, and vandalism.

In despair John stood and addressed the group: "Hi, I'm John, and I'm an alcoholic." He told his story and poured out his desperate anguish about his son.

When he sat down, Pete, a regular at the meeting, tapped John on the shoulder. Pete is a street person, often seen pushing a shopping cart through downtown Corona, bumming money and cigarettes from whomever he can. The money is spent on cheap wine to dull his pain and speed to keep him going. John had been hit up for money many times before by Pete. That's what John thought was going to happen this time, and given the heaviness of his heart it really irritated him.

He tried to ignore Pete, but Pete persisted. "John, John!" He tapped his shoulder again. "John, John, can I talk to you?"

Finally John turned around. "What do you want?"

"John, can we go outside? I need to show you something."

Reluctantly John muttered "OK" and steeled himself to resist the inevitable request for money. He headed for the door with Pete trailing behind.

They stood outside on the Sixth Street sidewalk with morning commuters rushing by. Pete said, "John, I want to tell you something about your boy."

"What about him?"

"Well, first I need to tell you about me. I grew up in a great family. My mom and dad were really proud of me. My dad thought that I should join the Navy like he had done to get some experience and educational benefits. So I did. The whole family came to my graduation from boot camp.

"My ship went into a Mexican port one weekend. I took shore leave with my buddies, and we smoked some pot. We were caught, and I received a dishonorable discharge. When I called my dad and told him what had happened, he said, 'Don't come home.' Then he and Mom stopped taking my calls. It's been years, and they've never talked to me again.

"But John, it doesn't have to be that way. Read this." Out of the pocket of his ragged, dirty jacket Pete produced a tattered paperback New Testament. He licked his grimy thumb, opened to a page, and handed it to John with a finger pointed to the starting place.

John read a passage that begins: "Then Jesus continued, 'There was a man who had two sons . . .'" He read about the younger son who couldn't wait for the father to die but took his inheritance and blew it on hookers and hard, fast living. He read about the son's hunger for corn husks and starvation for the love of the father. He read about the practiced speech and calculated effort of the son to get the father just to give him a place with the hired hands. He read about the father's unrestrained hug of forgiveness, the kiss of restored intimacy, and the big "welcome home" celebration. He read about the resentful elder brother who couldn't control his cold anger that hard work and good deeds didn't buy him a monopoly on the love of the father to the exclusion and disqualification of his shameful and shamed sibling. John read the concluding words of the father: "We had to celebrate and be glad, because this brother of yours was dead and is alive again; he was lost and is found" (Luke 15:11-32).

John looked up to see tears streaming down Pete's cheeks. Pete said, "John, you just gotta love him. You just gotta love your boy."

I never cease to marvel at the transformation of Jesus from a precocious carpenter's son in the rough and tough environs of Nazareth to the tender Savior who said: "As the Father has loved me, so have I loved you. Now live in my love" (John 15:9, NIV).

When Jesus was baptized He came up out of the water of the Jordan to see the heavens torn apart over His head and the Spirit descending like a dove on Him. He heard His Father's voice speaking the deepest truth to Him: "You are my Son, the Beloved; with you I am well pleased" (Mark 1:10, 11).

The next time He came home to Nazareth His grace and authority shocked His neighbors and friends. They said, "Isn't this Joseph's son? What's gotten into Him?" (see Luke 4:20-30). They couldn't handle the difference in Him and tried to kill Him.

In the last week of His life the chief priests and elders demanded to know His authority for His teaching and healing and who gave Him the authority. Jesus said He would tell them if they could answer this question: "Did the baptism of John come from heaven, or was it of human origin?" (Matthew 21:25). In that moment, in that question, Jesus recalled the source of His ministry—the fact that He was the Beloved of His Father. Knowing He was loved, He was free to live in love. In that freedom, Jesus loved us. "I am in my Father, and you in me, and I in you." "As the Father has loved me, so I have loved you; abide in my love. . . . No one has greater love than this, to lay down one's life for one's friends" (John 14:20; 15:9-13).

Brennan Manning writes: "The heart of the Father was Jesus' hiding place, a strong protective space where God was near, where the desert intimacy was renewed, where trust, love, and self-awareness never died but were continually rekindled. In times of opposition, rejection, hatred, and danger he retreated to that hiding place where he was loved. In times of weakness and fear a strength and mighty perseverance were born there. In the face of mounting incomprehension and mistrust, the Father alone understood him. 'No one knows who the Son is except the Father' (Luke 10:22). The Pharisees plotted secretly to destroy him; fair-weather friends shifted their allegiance; one disciple denied him and another betrayed him; but nothing could remove Jesus from his Father's love" (*The Gentle Revolutionaries* [Denville, N.J.: Dimension Books, 1976], pp. 84, 85).

What about you?

You are the beloved child of God through Jesus Christ! "But to all who received him, who believed in his name, he gave power to become children of God" (John 1:12). Believe Him!

TWELVE

Pure Religion

A landlord shocks a lawyer and his widowed client by a selfless display of Christian charity during a settlement discussion.

My mom, who never met a stranger, has a favorite Bible text: "Religion that is pure and undefiled before God, the Father, is this: to care for orphans and widows in their distress, and to keep oneself unstained by the world" (James 1:27). She has a radical, egalitarian Christianity founded on the belief that Christ calls us to help whoever needs help when and where they need help if it is in our capacity to do so. Her affinity is for the underdog in every situation.

Her son grew up to be an establishment defense attorney. I have met plenty of strangers and rarely encounter underdogs in my professional life. But even jaded, cynical lawyers can be surprised by grace. . . .

A woman and her three daughters came to me to incorporate their family business. They had moved 3,000 miles with their husband and father to establish the business. He died suddenly, leaving them to carry on, overwhelmed by the demands of business and grief. After incorporation they pooled what was left of their savings and bought a house. It was a "for sale by owner" deal with a "wraparound" deed of trust. They would pay the seller, and the seller would see that his lender was paid. This was a common practice in California real estate, the seller said. He seemed very knowledgeable and considerate. He had papers for the house that looked authentic. He told them they could save money by not going through an escrow. For the first time in their lives, mother and daughters negotiated and bought a house.

They made their payments faithfully for several months. Then I received a call from the mother. A man had come to the door, saying he was the owner of the house. He said he hadn't been receiving his rental payments and had come to see his tenant. The tenant was the erstwhile seller to my clients. He and his wife had taken the $25,000 down payment and had long since disappeared. The true owner of the house, a college professor named Ray McMurtry, wanted to sell the house. My clients were bewildered and facing eviction. McMurtry agreed to meet them at my office to discuss the problem.

The mother came alone. She was nervous. I was very concerned. Experience with California real estate scams told me that she and the daughters probably had no rights against the owner. They would likely lose their home and savings. I prayed with her that God would protect her family and bring justice to the situation.

McMurtry walked in. We exchanged business cards. He was a professor of education at a nearby Christian university.

We sat around my law firm's conference table. I told him how my clients had purchased the house. McMurtry told me the tenant was a member of his church who had seemed trustworthy when he rented the house. The home was an investment for McMurtry and his wife for their retirement. They had planned to sell it. He produced a deed and a title report proving his ownership. Then he said something to my client that snapped my head up from looking at my legal pad.

"I'm not going to throw you out of the house. You're a widow. You know I have an obligation to you."

"What did you say?" I asked.

"I said, 'Your client's a widow. I have an obligation to see that she does not lose the roof over her head.'"

"In my experience, sir, that is not the reaction of most property owners in your situation."

McMurtry shrugged. Then he proposed a lease-purchase plan in which the payments of my clients would be applied toward the purchase of the home.

I called McMurtry the next day. "I want to thank you for demonstrating mercy," I told him.

"Isn't that what a Christian is supposed to do?" he asked matter-of-factly.

"Yes, but almost no one follows through."

"I just do what I can," he said.

"Well, you sure surprised this lawyer."

He was true to his word. It cost his wife and him a lot of money. Years later a friend of mine who knows this story brought it up to McMurtry. "Oh, that" was all he said.

Jesus never prescribed a uniform or a hairstyle for His followers. He didn't give them a motto or a formula to wear on a T-shirt. He left us only one valid indicator to identify His disciples. "In the same way I loved you, you love one another. This is how everyone will recognize that you are my disciples—when they see the love you have for each other" (John 13:34, 35, Message). Ray McMurtry is a disciple. He makes me want to be one too.

THIRTEEN

The Fledgling

*A father and son experience a moment of grace
during a transition in their relationship.*

"D id you hear that?" Dad called to me across the yard.

I straightened up from my work on my dusty VW and looked at him blankly. "Hear what?"

"Listen," he said. "Up there in the eucalyptus."

I heard nothing but the mooing cows in the neighbor's pasture.

"What is it?" I wanted to get back to my car. It was getting late, and I had places to go and friends to see that night.

Before Dad could speak again I heard it. Piercing the quiet air of the valley came the raucous scream of a hawk—startling, but haunting. Again it shrilled, and it was answered by a softer-pitched cry.

Dad leaned his hoe against a beanpole and walked toward me through his garden. "The old one is teaching the young ones to fly. They must have a nest up there somewhere. Let's walk up there and have a look."

I was away at college nine months of the year. In the summer Dad and I worked together during the day, but I was usually visiting friends in the evening. Free times and walks with my father were rare.

I guess I should go, I thought to myself. *Then maybe he and Mom will stop complaining that I don't spend enough time at home.*

"OK, let's go," I said, wiping my hands on an oily rag.

We walked in silence around the old barn, intently watching the eucalyptus at the mouth of the arroyo. We didn't bother to open the pasture gate. I parted the barbed-wire strands for him, and he did for me, and we walked on through the pasture.

Late-afternoon sun filtered through the oaks on the ridge behind the pasture and drizzled a gentle patchwork on the green-watered slope. As we walked, killdeers started up from their feeding and, piping their thin wails, skittered on ahead of us before stopping to bob nervously on skinny legs.

On the other side of the field at the arroyo's mouth we passed the trough. The old bathtub was only half full. It had been a hot July. The worn, hoof-pocked hollow around the tub smelled rich and dank of moss and algae.

We opened the upper gate and quietly entered the arroyo. The tall silver trunks stretched up stiffly from the dry sandy wash. A slight breeze from Monterey Bay lightly rustled the long-fingered leaves.

"Where are they?" I asked, breaking our silence. Even as I spoke, another scream broke harshly above us.

"Up there," Dad whispered.

On a twisted, rough-barked limb, maybe 75 feet up, sat a huge red-tailed hawk.

"That's the biggest one I've ever seen," I whispered back.

"There's the mate." My father pointed at the sky. I craned my neck. In the blue above the grove another hawk gracefully swept in a spiraling circle.

"Where are the little ones?" I asked.

"Over there across the gully." I followed his gaze up to the crown on the tallest eucalyptus, where a jumble of twisted sticks and bark were packed in the crotch of two limbs. I couldn't see what was in the nest.

"Accommodations aren't too comfortable, are they?" I murmured.

Dad chuckled. "That's just like where we found Old Charlie." Long ago, in his boyhood, Dad and my uncles had had a pet hawk. They caught him in a cottonwood by their swimming hole in the San Joaquin Valley. They named him Charlie and raised him on cottage cheese and the jackrabbits they shot with their .22s. The stories of their adventures with Charlie had been my favorites when I was little.

The parent hawks continued their sharp wheedling. Suddenly there was a tumbling blur at the nest and then another. The young hawks plummeted from the branch until it seemed they were going to crash. Then the instinct of flight took over and the two balls of bronze fluff began to flutter, floundering to stay up. The parents swooped down to them and egged the fledglings above the branches and into the evening blue above. I watched until I lost sight of them through the leaves. Turning, I found Dad looking at me, smiling a little wistfully.

"It's getting dark," he said hurriedly. "Mom'll have supper ready."

We strolled out of the arroyo into the pasture. The forested hills on the far side of the valley glowed with the sunlight above the shadows. We walked down through the piping killdeers to the house.

The barbed wire protested with a squeak as I lifted it for Dad. On the other side he held it for me.

"Thanks, Dad."

He grinned and squeezed my shoulders with his strong fingers.

"Sure, son."

Together we went to supper.

FOURTEEN

Of Rattlesnakes and Waterfalls

*Fear causes us to lose our perspective
and our view of God's goodness.*

I write to you of rattlesnakes and waterfalls. I write to you of a revelation of grace.

The guidebook says: "With five tiers and a total drop of 150 feet, Tenaja Falls is the most interesting geographical feature in the San Mateo Canyon wilderness. In late winter and spring, water coursing down the polished rock produces a kind of soothing music not widely heard in this somewhat dry corner of the Santa Ana Mountains" (Jerry Schad, *Afoot and Afield in Orange County* [Berkeley, Calif.: Wilderness Press, 1988], p. 104). Rock and water in combination are irresistible to me. I wanted to see this waterfall in a remote wilderness area about 40 miles from my home.

I first traversed a rough wilderness track eroded by heavy winter rains. This was no problem for my trusty Toyota Land Cruiser.

After reaching the trail head, I crossed a rain-swollen creek and made my way up a rocky, brush-choked canyon floor toward where I thought the falls would be. It was there that I gave serious thought to the rattlesnakes.

Rattlesnakes are a fact of the trail in Southern California. The Indians drew pictures of them on the rocks. Spanish and early United States explorers wrote of their dangers in expedition journals. I have encountered them at 7,700 feet on mountain ridges and on city streets.

An estimated 300 rattlesnake bites a year occur in Southern California.

The snakes are most active in temperatures of 75-90 degrees between early spring and midfall. According to the same guidebook where I found the directions to Tenaja Falls, I found this reference:

"Rattlesnakes are fairly common in brushy, rocky and streamside habitats from coast to mountains. . . . Watch carefully where you put your feet, and especially your hands, during rattlesnake season. In brushy or rocky areas where sight distance is short, try to make your presence known from afar. Tread with heavy footfalls, or use a stick to bang against rocks or bushes. Rattlesnakes will pick up the vibrations and buzz (unmistakably) before you get too close for comfort" (*ibid.*, p. 9).

I carry a long English yew thumb stick (I slip my thumb over a fork at the top) when I hike. I've carried it for 18 years, and my spouse and friends know that I want to be buried with it when I die. In the canyon brush I proceeded carefully, probing ahead with my stick.

It was 11:00 a.m. when I started. The temperature was about 80 degrees. It was late March, the time when rattlesnakes come out of hibernation, hungry and irritated. My desire to see the falls in season struggled against my concern about snakes. The willow, lilac, bunch grass, coastal sage, coyote brush, nettle, mule tail, manzanita, scrub oak, and poison oak (yikes!) were so thick that I could barely see my boot tops. My eyes were glued to the ground ahead.

Looking down so much, I lost my bearings and ended up in a side ravine in thick, thick wild lilac higher than my head. I plunged on in the direction where I thought I would find the falls, but I could not see or even hear them.

After two hours of bush-whacking I came to a big sycamore log on a sandbar. I checked around the log for snakes and sat down to eat my lunch. Sitting down in the stillness, I realized how tense I was. The anxious watching was taking the joy away from the experience and had led me off the path. I spotted a faint but true trail on the opposite bank. My breathing relaxed, and the breeze was cool against my sweaty back. I prayed to God in thanks for the journey so far and for guidance on the trail ahead.

When I repacked my stuff I stood and slung the day pack over my shoulders. I picked up my stick and looked up the canyon. There, in a breathtaking cascade of sunlit silver spray, was Tenaja Falls. It had clearly been in my view for some time. Standing still, I could even hear its steady rush in the distance.

The care of my work washed from me in the gracious sight. I forgot my fear-filled fantasies.

In that instant a life truth was revealed to me. If I am intently focused on the possibility of the snakes, I will miss the wonderful shining waterfall. If my effort is directed toward avoiding the sting of death, I will miss the healing water of life.

Jesus spoke to His disciples about snakes with names such as wars and rebellions, earthquakes, famines, diseases, persecution, betrayal and hatred by loved ones, displacement, distress, wrath, paralyzing fear, and anxiety about the future. And when He told them about these dangers in answering their deepest concerns He also said: "Now when these things begin to take place, stand up and raise your heads, because your redemption is drawing near" (Luke 21:28).

Two of Jesus' followers didn't get the message. On a lonely journey home after their hopes were crushed at Golgotha, their eyes were looking along the road for the vipers of grief, disappointment, confusion, injustice, and the death of hope. Jesus Himself came near and went with them. They could not bring themselves to look up and recognize the grace of His resurrected presence. He began to explain the truth that would save them from the serpents of their fears. They were moved to invite Him to dinner with one of my favorite prayers: "Stay with us, because it is almost evening and the day is now nearly over" (Luke 24:29).

In the grace of the meal, they sat and rested. He blessed and broke the bread of their sustenance and gave it to them from His own nail-pierced hands. At that moment their eyes were opened wide to the recognition of Jesus, and their hearts burned with the revelation of His shining presence (verses 13-35).

You may be losing the bearings of your journey in the paralyzing fear of the snakes in the brush. Maybe the snake is the relationship that won't hold together, or the budget that won't balance. Perhaps you have a job that bleeds you rather than feeds you, or a child whose only contact with you is the coil and strike of angry words. Or are you facing the depression that masks the fear of inadequacy and failure, the shame of sin unconfessed, forgiveness withheld, or community betrayed. I pray for you and me the words of Psalm 80:19: "Restore us, O Lord God of hosts; let your face shine that we may be saved."

Right now if you look up with the eyes of your heart, there is a waterfall before you—a torrent of grace—the water of life flowing right out of the hard rock of your heart, flowing down into the brush-choked, snake-infested box canyon of your life. I do not make this stuff up! Jesus cries out, "Let anyone who is thirsty come to me, and let the one who believes in me drink. As the scripture has said, 'Out of the believer's heart shall flow rivers of living water'" (John 7:37, 38).

This is the call of grace, a guaranteed snake bite remedy: "Now when these things begin to take place"—the things you dread most and that threaten to rob you of eternity and hope—"stand up and raise your heads, because your redemption [the Son of man coming in a cloud with power and great glory] is drawing near" (Luke 21:28).

Jesus Christ, Son of the living God, have mercy on us. May we look up to see the sunlit glory of Your cascading grace. May we all bathe and play in its cleansing, healing pools and drops. We praise You, Jesus, for You have crushed the serpent that would destroy us beneath Your heel. You are our peace. Move from our heads into our hearts the certain knowledge that we are now safe to look up and enjoy You. We say our eternal Yes to You! Amen.

FIFTEEN

The Journey Without Baggage

*The Christlike life is a journey, but Jesus says
to leave your baggage at home.*

I have a physician friend named Dave. Some years ago we sat in our church's youth chapel while our congregation's leadership talked to us about what kind of pastor we should select to replace our previous pastor. He had resigned after a long battle over things I can't even remember.

Such analogies as "an orchestra conductor able to harmonize the members who play different instruments" were tossed around. Lists of qualities were proposed and discussed. People who didn't trust each other any farther than the aisle that divided them verbally edged their preferred traits up the list over the ideas of their adversaries. The temptation in such a situation is to opt for the innocuous and inoffensive.

When the meeting was over I told Dave: "I know one thing. I never again want to be part of the status quo. I want to be part of something that means something—that changes things, that changes me."

Dave said, "I know what you mean. I used to think that if I studied hard and went to medical school and did well, I would be comfortable. That wasn't it. Then I thought if I married and had a nice family and built a good practice and lived a good life, I would be comfortable. But that didn't do it. Then I thought if I developed a relationship with Jesus, I would be comfortable. But that didn't happen. Now I know that I'll never be comfortable, and that is OK, because we aren't meant to be comfortable on this earth. We aren't intended to stay here."

A woman standing near us overheard Dave's remarks. She was a rising star in a well-known multilevel marketing program. She apparently couldn't believe what she was hearing and burst out, "But Dave, think of all the good you can do with the money you make as a doctor!"

His reply was quick: "But it's not my money, and that's the thing about it."

Dave's words that night eight years ago have inspired and encouraged me ever since. It is deceitful and presumptuous to think that when we do enough and earn enough we can share some of it with God. It all belongs to God. Ownership is a concept alien to grace. We are stewards. Followers of Christ are homeless.

"Sometimes we think we would like to just settle down, turn off the thoughts or images, the feelings and emotions, and find some hole or nest where we could simply be. But that is not the lot of the follower of Christ. 'The Son of Man has no place to lay his head' (Matthew 8:20 [NIV]). We belong to the pilgrim people of God. We are ever on the journey. There is always room for more growth. The Lord wants to lead us ever more deeply into himself, into the mysteries of his love, and all of this is beyond our thoughts and images, our feelings and emotions" (M. Basil Pennington, *Call to the Center* [New City Press, 1995], p. 80).

Hebrews 11 recounts the faithfulness of Abel, Enoch, Noah, Abraham, and Sarah. "Each one of these people of faith died not yet having in hand what was promised, but still believing. How did they do it? They saw it way off in the distance, waved their greeting, and accepted the fact that they were transients in this world. People who live this way make it plain that they are looking for their true home. If they were homesick for the old country, they could have gone back any time they wanted. But they were after a far better country than that—*heaven* country. You can see why God is so proud of them, and has a City waiting for them" (Hebrews 11:13-16, Message).

The apostle James says that our conflicts and our violence originate in our desire to own things (James 4:1-6). If we own things, we want to stay. We forget the provision of God and seek our own self-preservation. Jesus spoke the hard truth that commitment to Him and to no one else, including the most intimate of family and friends, is the way of discipleship. Jesus eschewed person, place, and thing as means of salvation. He taught that He and He alone is "the way, and the truth, and the life" (John 14:6). He said, "And I, when I am lifted up from the earth, will draw all people to myself" (John 12:32). The life and death challenge to us as the people of God is whether we trust Jesus enough to depend on Him and Him alone as the catalyst for the growth of the body.

A friend of mine, Ed, read Paul's letter to the Galatians through every day for a month. The Galatians were a people who accepted the gospel of Jesus only to be talked out of it by spiritual bean counters who told them, "You don't have anything if you can't measure it, count it, or hold it." When their hands were full of this spiritual baggage the Galatians began to compare themselves and each other, and they lost grace. Ed's synopsis of the letter after his month of reading was this: "It's Jesus, stupid."

This is easily forgotten when we institute our communities of faith. First, God calls us to community and we learn and grow in the fellowship. But the temptation comes to preserve the community at all costs, even obedience to God. We succumb to the original deceit that "good" is something we can know and possess ourselves rather than something received from God (see Genesis 3:6). At that point we cross the spiritual line from stewardship to ownership and begin exercising the prerogatives of ownership to preserve our property rights. In claiming ownership we cease to be a community of faith, because we are announcing our independence and our decision to set up camp where we are. To do this often requires the financial support and efforts of those who do not share commitment to a sovereign God, but instead embrace our camp as an inherently good place where they would like to stay for their own purposes. How easy it is to forget Jesus' slicing words to a wealthy, powerful seeker after goodness: "Only God is truly good" (Luke 18:19, NLT). Those who seek not to establish themselves as a force for good, but who instead heed the call of God to move on are written off as radicals, dilettantes and ne'er-do-wells. At that point the life-bringing arteries of a movement of God harden into the congested heart failure of an organization requiring artificial life support.

The writings of theologians Stanley Hauerwas and William Willimon challenge me on these points:

"The Gospels make wonderfully clear that the disciples had not the foggiest idea of what they had gotten into when they followed Jesus. With a simple 'follow me,' Jesus invited ordinary people to come out and be part of an adventure, a journey that kept surprising them at every turn in the road. It is no coincidence that the Gospel writers chose to frame the gospel in terms of a journey: 'And then Jesus went to,' 'From there he took his disciples to,' 'From that time he began to teach them that. . . .'

"When Jesus commissioned his disciples and sent them out (Luke 10:1-24), he told them to take no bag, purse, or sandals—the sorts of accessories required for most journeys. Here was a journey in which they were to take only confidence in his empowerment. The story ends with the disciples coming back, utterly surprised that the same power of good, which they had experienced in Jesus, was also working in them (verses 17-24). When it comes to confirmation of the truth of the gospel, disciples are often more surprised than anyone else when, wonder of wonders, what Jesus promises, Jesus really does give.

"In a way, although Jesus unburdened the disciples of so much of the baggage the world considers essential, he did not relieve them of all burdens. He relieved them of false baggage so he could lay upon them even more demanding burdens. For in laying upon them the necessity to trust not their possessions but only him, Jesus showed them that here was a journey which required the cultivation of certain *virtues*. One should not start out on a dangerous journey without being equipped for the dangers that one may face. So, in any good adventure story, we find a constant testing of the traveler's character and, during the testing, a transformation in the character of the adventurer. The quest requires the adventurer to rely upon and develop his or her virtues in ever-new ways.

"To launch out on a journey is to move toward some *goal*. Of course, in the journey of faith, we have no clear idea of what our end will be except that it shall be, in some form, true and complete friendship with God. For now, our daily experiences of testing and confirmation of that friendship sustain us. Perhaps this explains why Jesus' ethic was so thoroughly eschatological—an ethic bound up with his proclamation of the end of history. Ethics is a function of the *telos,* the end. It makes all the difference in the world how one regards the end of the world, 'end,' not so much in the sense of its final breath, but 'end' in the sense of the purpose, the goal, the result" (Stanley Hauerwas and William H. Willimon, *Resident Aliens* [Nashville: Abingdon Press, 1989], pp. 49-62).

Jesus is both the journey and its end in verity. "'I am the Alpha and the Omega,' says the Lord God, who is and who was and who is to come, the Almighty" (Revelation 1:8). We come at His invitation and go at His command. We rest in His arms. We travel light with Him.

SIXTEEN

Keep That Hand Up

*A child's reaction to an accident in a backyard
swimming pool exposes the essentials of saving faith.*

Our family attended a pool party for a friend graduating from high school. Our son, Andrew, then 4 years old, splashed in the shallow end of the pool in noisy play with the other kids.

Patricia and I kept an eye on him. He had had swimming lessons, but you can't be too careful. My friend Randy and I talked, and somehow as we stood poolside I turned my back to the water. Suddenly Randy broke off in midsentence and rushed past me to the pool. He reached into the deep end and to my surprise pulled out a sputtering Andrew.

Andrew had slowly slipped down the pool edge until he was in the deep end. Then he let go and sank like a stone. Randy, a watchful PE teacher, saw him go down.

Patricia asked Andrew, "Are you OK?"

"Yes, Mommy. I went down in the water and couldn't do anything, so I just held up my hand and waited for somebody to come for me. And he did."

There are many things that my son, Andrew, brings to life for me, most significantly the gospel. The author of Hebrews defined faith as "the assurance of things hoped for, the conviction of things not seen" (Hebrews 11:1). Andrew, in over his head in deep water, had the assurance of a salvation that he could not see but believed would arrive.

Saving faith is exactly like this: a realization of our dire predicament, a recognition that we cannot help ourselves, a belief that there is one who can and will save us, and a hand outstretched to receive that gift of salvation.

It is that simple, but we are human, and the harrowing circumstances of our life in a broken world frighten us. Andrew suffered a fear of water for some time after that incident even though he had more swimming lessons.

One hot summer day I took him swimming. He stepped into the shallow end wearing a life jacket. He refused to venture across the pool to play with me.

"Come on," I said, "you can do it."

"No."

"Oh sure you can. You're a good swimmer."

"I don't want to."

"Daddy won't let anything happen to you, and it will be fun."

"But I don't want to drown. That's the thing!"

That is the "thing" indeed. On one hand he believed that his loving daddy wouldn't let him sink. On the other hand the water was real and could swallow him up.

This is how a desperate man came to stand on the lower slope of the Mount of Transfiguration and cry out to Jesus, "I believe; help my unbelief!" (Mark 9:24).

Jesus heard the cry of the conflicted man, broke off the theological dialogue with him, and healed the man's son on the spot. When you are actually in the water or the mess or the struggle or whatever, all the Bible verses and Helen Steiner Rice platitudes in the world won't pull you out. It is why Patricia says, "No one should be given a book on how to endure suffering when they are truly suffering." To read or listen to an intellectual discourse on why the thing that sends adrenaline coursing through your veins or tears your heart in pieces is really good for you most often pulls us into deeper despair. Our heart does not follow the lead of our head.

Andrew dives and swims with abandon now. He came back to this grace in the love and pool play of his friends. The greater joy of relationship in the freedom of the water gradually removed his self-consciousness.

The journey to the heart of the kingdom of God takes time. The power of sin and our self-possession are deeply rooted and very deceptive in their reach and hold. We wonder, *Why am I not spared this or that? If God really loved me, wouldn't this pain have stopped a long time ago? If Christ really cared, would this be happening?*

We inch along the pool edge thinking we can go farther and farther into the deep water and still get back. This is why there are such things as deathbed confessions of faith. It takes that long for some of us to realize that we are in over our heads and that there is nothing to be done but hold up our hand to the Christ who we believe can pull us out. Some never get to that point or pass it by without even a wave.

It is exactly this point of recognition of our futility upon which eternity pivots. Our mortality is inevitable. Is there a realistic hope for immortality, and with whom is that hope to be found? In answer I offer the story I heard Brennan Manning tell of a Bahamian family whose home caught on fire in the night. The father and mother shepherded the children outside. In the front yard they counted heads and realized that their 4-year-old son was missing. The father ran back to the house, shouting the name of his boy.

A little voice was heard over the crackle of the flames. "I'm up here, Daddy."

The father looked up. The child was silhouetted against the flames in a second-story window. Smoke billowed out the window, obscuring the little boy from moment to moment.

"Jump," the father yelled. "Jump, boy!"

"I can't see you, Daddy!" was the terrified reply.

"It's OK to jump," the father called back, "because I can see you."

O child of grace, your Abba this very moment has your name penned in the palm of His hand and an exact count of every hair on your head. You can hold up that hand for help in the blessed assurance that Abba will grasp it. The apostle John wrote:

"We have seen and do testify that the Father has sent his Son as the Savior of the world. God abides in those who confess that Jesus is the Son of God, and they abide in God. So we have known and believe the love that God has for us" (1 John 4:14-16). The water may be deep, but keep that hand up. Someone who loves you, and you want no one else, is coming to pull you out.

SEVENTEEN

What She Did for Love

An obscure and disgraceful episode in the life of David demonstrates the essential difference between authority and power.

C onsider these statements:

"Not by might, nor by power, but by my spirit, says the Lord of hosts" (Zechariah 4:6).

"Authority is the ability to lead, and we depend on it for virtually everything we try to achieve. Our authority is built on very different qualities than our power, on the attractiveness of our values, on the force of our example, on the credibility of our commitments, and on our willingness to work with and stand by others" (Samuel "Sandy" Berger, U.S. national security adviser, 1999).

Let's contemplate the difference between power and authority.

Her name was Rizpah. She was a concubine of King Saul, to whom she bore two sons. Saul died in battle with the Philistines, and his weak son Ish-bosheth came to rule 11 of the tribes of Israel. Saul's nemesis and God's chosen king, David, ruled Judah to the south.

The strong man of the kingdom was Saul's general, Abner. As Ish-bosheth was weak, Abner gained in strength in the royal household. To show himself as the heir to Saul's power, he began an affair with Rizpah, who had no power to protest. Ish-bosheth objected. "Why are you sleeping with my father's concubine?" he asked Abner (see 2 Samuel 3:7).

Abner responded with a self-righteous, angry tirade about his faithfulness to the memory and legacy of Saul. He ended by telling Ish-bosheth, "Just because you accuse me of an offense against this woman, I'll show you. I'll turn over everything left of Saul's kingdom to David (see verses 8-11).

Great treachery followed. Abner attempted to make good on his threat by going to David and turning over the kingdom, but after their meeting David's jealous thug of a general, Joab, assassinated Abner.

When Ish-bosheth heard that Abner was dead, he suffered a fearful paralysis of nerve and spirit. He was assassinated in bed by two of his subjects thinking to curry favor with David. Violence and war followed until David conquered the whole kingdom and established Jerusalem as his capital. He then went to work through a combination of military strength and political dealing to consolidate his power.

Nothing more was heard of Rizpah for several years, that is, until . . .

A three-year famine afflicted Israel. David asked God what caused it. God replied, "There is bloodguilt on Saul and on his house, because he put the Gibeonites to death" (2 Samuel 21:1). The Gibeonites were a remnant of the Amorites, a people that Israel had sworn to protect when they entered the land of Canaan. Saul broke that promise when he tried to exterminate the Gibeonites in an attempt to purify Israel. God expects His people to honor their word even when the result seems less than God would want (Psalm 15:4). Saul's attempt at ethnic cleansing led to disaster for the Gibeonites through bloodshed and the Israelites through starvation.

David did not wait for God to give him instruction on how to solve the problem. He went to the Gibeonites and asked them what could make up for the harm done them. They told him, "You couldn't pay us enough money to make up for this, and we don't want to kill Israelites."

David asked them, "What do you want me to do for you?"

"This is between us and Saul because he tried to destroy us. Hand over seven of his sons and we will impale them on poles on the mountain."

David had made a promise to protect the children of Saul's son Jonathan, so David spared Jonathan's son Mephibosheth. He took instead five sons of Saul's daughter Merab and Rizpah's two sons by Saul. He handed them over to the Gibeonites, who impaled them on the first day of the harvest so that looking up from the fields they could see the corpses and know that Gibeah had been avenged.

Rizpah took sackcloth and spread it out on a rock beside the poles. Throughout the harvest and into the winter rains she kept vigil there, day and night, shooing away the vultures and wild animals that came to feed on the corpses of her sons and their nephews. It must have been horrific for her. We have seen scenes like this in the television pictures from Bosnia and Kosovo. A woman, deprived of home and love by the intrigues and power games of arrogant and violent men, now confronting the death by torture of her children innocent of any crime except being born into families burning with ancient prejudices.

Where is the grace in this? Rizpah is the grace. She did the only thing she could do, and it was everything. No mother ever gave birth that her children should suffer this fate. And when, in spite of mother's love and royal birth, evil ravaged them anyway, she kept them precious in memory and honored in rest by refusing to let the indignity visited upon them in life follow them into death. She had committed to bring them into the world, and she stayed with them as their life ended and beyond.

Rizpah's path took her from a position of privileged mistress of wealthy and powerful men through the disruption of war and political deal-making to the Palestinian mountainside where her sacrificial love transformed this squalid story into a testament of the gospel. It brings her sons to life in our memory nearly 3,000 years later. Hers was a pure act of grace; a gift of herself for no purpose but love.

Her vigil came to the attention of David and rebuked him. God had not told him to practice human sacrifice to end the famine. David gave the Gibeonites what they wanted in a political act to no good result. Word of Rizpah's love, transcending famine, politics, horror, and fear shamed David to action. He had the bodies of the young men cut down and gathered up the bones of the rest of Saul's family and gave them a state burial. Grace triumphed over disgrace. The authentic authority of love proved stronger than political power and death. It was only then, when love, not power, had its way, that God ended the famine in Israel (2 Samuel 21:14).

This story reveals the difference between power and authority. Abraham Lincoln said that the true test of a man is not how he handles adversity but what he does when given power. David, given power, went to God to discern the problem but went to his own strength for the answer. He had the power to take five children and two grandchildren of his defeated predecessor and sacrifice them for a political solution to a spiritual problem. But those seven young men were the sons of mothers. They were flesh and blood. In the raw exercise of power, whether in war or peace, flesh and blood become commodities for the schemes of the powerful. "Might does not make right" is a concept we learn in childhood but easily forget as adults.

I am in my twenty-second year as an attorney and administrator. I am privileged to represent religious organizations, educational institutions, and hospitals. These are nonprofit organizations intended for helpful solutions to the basic needs of humankind. Every day in such a place one given authority to lead must deal with the temptation of power. Eugene Peterson wrote: "Because leadership is an exercise of authority, it can easily become an exercise of power. But the minute it does that, it starts to damage both the leader and the led" (Introduction to 2 Corinthians, *The Message*). This is what happened to David. The seduction of leadership is to do something just because you can do it. Doing something usually turns out to be doing something to someone. We exercise *power* when we use someone else to make our point. We exercise *authority* when we convince someone to agree with our point. The authentic difference is found in love and the leading of the Holy Spirit.

Henri Nouwen addressed the difference between the coercion of power and the authority of love in a passage that has fundamentally changed my thinking about my own leadership:

"What makes the temptation of power so seemingly irresistible? Maybe it is that power offers an easy substitute for the hard task of love. It seems easier to be God than to love God, easier to control people than to love people, easier to own life than to love life. Jesus asks, 'Do you love Me?' We ask, 'Can we sit at Your right hand and Your left hand in Your kingdom?' (Matthew 20:21). Ever since the snake said, 'The day you eat of this tree your eyes will be open and you will be like God, knowing good and evil' (Genesis 3:5), we have been tempted to replace love with power. Jesus lived that temptation in the most agonizing way from the desert to the cross. The long painful history of the church is the history of people ever and again tempted to choose power over love, control over the cross, being a leader over being led. Those who resisted this temptation to the end and thereby give us hope are the true saints.

"One thing is clear to me: the temptation of power is greatest when intimacy is a threat. Much Christian leadership is exercised by people who do not know how to develop healthy, intimate relationships and have opted for power and control instead. Many Christian empire-builders have been people unable to give and receive love" (*In the Name of Jesus* [New York: Crossroad, 1989], pp. 59, 60).

About a thousand years after Rizpah's stand for love against power, another Son was nailed to a cross on a Palestinian hillside by power brokers.

The night before He died it was observed that "having loved his own who were in the world, he loved them to the end" (John 13:1). He demonstrated it by washing the feet of His disciples, including those who before the next morning would betray Him for power and flee from Him for fear of power. But He chose the authority of love over power. When He finished washing and drying their feet, He asked, "Do you know what I have done to you? You call me Teacher and Lord—and you are right, for that is what I am. So if I, your Lord and Teacher have washed your feet, you also ought to wash one another's feet. For I have set you an example, that you also should do as I have done to you" (verses 12-15).

Rizpah did not live and Jesus did not die in vain. Live and love under the faithful authority of Jesus Christ by His grace alone.

EIGHTEEN

Night Work in a Holy Place

*Not every cathedral is a church; not all ministers are clergy
—lessons learned in a neonatal intensive-care unit.*

The sliding security doors of the Loma Linda University Medical Center open, releasing me into the freshness of a new night. A gibbous moon hangs low over the palm trees along the street. Venus shines bright to the west, the direction of my home—faithful reminders of the world that continues outside.

The meetings are ended for the day, the contracts reviewed for now. The immediate future lies heavy in the soft-sided briefcase in my left hand. Depositing the case in my car's back seat and closing the door, I turn and gaze back across the parking lot at the towers and ramparts of the giant institution that I serve as legal counsel. My eyes rest on the third row of lighted windows.

During the day patients, vendors, clerks, nurses, medical residents, technicians, students, physicians, visitors, case managers, engineers, lawyers, and administrators throng the hospital in a Dickensian scene. The business of health care is being done.

At night we money changers leave the temple, and the liturgy of healing commences. This is when I think the medical center does its best work. The tests are completed and the diagnosis made. The plans of care have been charted. The vigil of healing commences. Voices hush, nurses move from bedside to bedside in the consistent rhythms of care, in the perseverance of service. Seventy-two infants fill every bed in the neonatal intensive-care unit on the third floor. They are very ill. The care they receive must be constant and focused, a labor of love on the precipitous perimeter between life and death. It is God's work. The medical center's stated mission is "to continue the healing ministry of Jesus Christ."

These patients are almost impossibly tiny. They represent the best part of their mothers and fathers. They are dreams struggling for fulfillment, a match light cupped against the wind. Right at the start, when all should be delight and wonder, something has gone terribly wrong—a pancreas producing too much insulin eating away the flesh; the rampaging cells of leukemia; hearts with holes seeping life away with every beat; intestines where lungs should be breathing free. Wonder turns to unbearable tension; delight turns to dread in the acidic reduction of terror. Prayers of family and loved ones grope through the darkness for handholds of hope. Into these desperate moments enter the nurses and physicians, intervenors of grace, whose exacting and holy vocation is to support the smallest and the weakest in their grasp for life. This is heart- and soul-risking work requiring exhausting concentration. These patients cannot describe their symptoms. Every sign must be read and interpreted without the communication of the patient. No tracker in the wilderness has a more difficult challenge.

Standing alone in the parking lot, I look up toward the NICU, and I see through the eyes of my heart these ministers of healing moving from crib to crib, lifting holy hands—caressing, adjusting, holding through the night. It was there that I had watched a mother and 3-week-old daughter reach out to hold each other's hand. The baby girl rested high in a blanketed nest on a machine that warmed and circulated the blood her own weak heart could not move adequately and breathed the breaths her pneumonia-ravaged lungs could not breathe on their own. It was an altar of sorts, and we stood before it in semicircle—the physicians, the nurses, and their lawyer, who is learning the ways of this place. The baby's eyes were bright, and she smiled as her fingers touched her mom.

How can it be? I thought. Beside me stood the kind neonatologist, whose own heart seems, of necessity, enlarged for the compassion and competence it must hold in balance. "She looks so good—how long can it go on like this?" I asked him. He whispered, "The lungs and heart are really gone. Her other organs are shutting down. It would be over now except we all see exactly what you see, and we don't quit."

I moved on through the unit, pausing crib by crib, observing the care and hearing stories of successes, crises, and heartbreaks. Moms rocked those babies who could be held and watched over those who couldn't. Nurses navigated gracefully amid a tangle of tubes and wires and blinking lights. All the while, my beeper vibrated urgently at my waist in message and duplicate message. When I finally emerged into the hallway outside I returned the page. "Where were you?" an administrator demanded. "We need to talk about the contract."

"I'm sorry, but I was in the NICU. I thought it was kind of irreverent to stop and return the page."

"What do you mean?"

"I mean that is a sacred place. Life and death are happening in there, and I don't think it is appropriate to interrupt the staff and say, 'Do you have a phone I can use? I need to tend to some business.'"

"Do you really feel like that?" he asked.

"I really feel like that."

Every night since then when I've left the medical center in darkness, I've paused and looked up at the lights on the third floor.

In the Jerusalem Temple, worship was a 24-hour-a-day, seven-day-a-week circumstance. It was led by professionals, Levites, who ministered prayers and praise to a God whose presence was above all and yet so near and so needed as the source of life itself. They worked in shifts. Through the night some of them were always on duty, doing as good a job at 3:00 a.m. as the day shift did at 3:00 p.m. They sang a song of devotion as they performed their faithful service keeping the light in the darkness.

> Come, bless the Lord, all you servants of the Lord,
>   who stand by night in the house of the Lord!
> Lift up your hands to the holy place,
>   and bless the Lord.
>
> May the Lord, maker of heaven and earth,
>   bless you from Zion (Psalm 134).

It is this prayer that rises in my heart in the parking lot beneath the third-floor NICU. It is this prayer that I pray for those within before I drive home. There are cathedrals that are not churches. There are ministers who are not clergy. The healing ministry of Jesus Christ continues this night in this place. "He who keeps Israel will neither slumber nor sleep" (Psalm 121:3).

NINETEEN

Letting My Donkey Go

God requires everything, and devotion withholds nothing.

Jesus sent two disciples, saying to them, 'Go into the village ahead of you, and immediately you will find a donkey tied, and a colt with her; untie them and bring them to me. If anyone says anything to you, just say this, "The Lord needs them." And he will send them immediately.' This took place to fulfill what had been spoken through the prophet, saying, 'Tell the daughter of Zion, Look, your king is coming to you, humble, and mounted on a donkey, and on a colt, the foal of a donkey.' The disciples went and did as Jesus directed them, they brought the donkey and the colt, and put their cloaks on them, and he sat on them" (Matthew 21:1-7).

Transportation? Beast of burden? Net worth? Prized possession? Family pet? What did the donkey and the colt represent to their anonymous owner? Was he aware of the prophecy of the coming Messiah and his supporting role in its fulfillment? Or did he have that simple certainty of a Spirit-filled heart that "I and all that is mine are available to my Lord"?

What we do know is that his response was quick and unequivocal—the response of a faithful steward, not an owner. It carries with it the sure scent of trust, obedience, and gratitude. The authentic sign of a heart gift is its dear cost, given willingly without question or negotiation. The donkey and colt were not bargaining chips. He released them into the unconditional current of grace and history. This gift was used by Christ to move on toward the salvation of the donkey's owner and us.

This story moves me. The challenge is whether I am willing to let go of all that I claim as mine to Christ—possessions; pets, whether people, ideas, or projects; burdens and the means I've devised for carrying them; my modus operandi. Am I willing to let go of my present—the donkey? Am I willing to let go of my expectation of what is to come—the colt? In the yield of such willingness is the kingdom of God to be found.

I don't care that the owner of the donkey was anonymous. I want to be like him. When the Lord says to me "I have need," whether of me or mine, I want the unquestioning heart and the generous soul of that man. May Christ move on and I never look back. What about you?

TWENTY

The Eyes of My Father

A father builds a bridge to pay for eye surgery for his child.

Annie Dillard wrote about the wonder of men and women given their sight through surgery after a lifetime of blindness.

"[Many] newly sighted people speak well of the world, and teach us how dull is our own vision. To one patient, a human hand, unrecognized is 'something bright and then holes.' Shown a bunch of grapes, a boy calls out, 'It is dark, blue and shiny . . . It isn't smooth, it has bumps and hollows.' A little girl visits a garden. 'She is greatly astonished, and can scarcely be persuaded to answer, stands speechless in front of the tree, which she only names on taking hold of it, and then as "the tree with the lights in it."' Some delight in their sight and give themselves over to the visual world. Of a patient just after her bandages were removed, her doctor writes, 'The first things to attract her attention were her own hands; she looked at them very closely, moved them repeatedly to and fro, bent and stretched the fingers, and seemed greatly astonished at the sight.' One girl was eager to tell her blind friend that 'men do not really look like trees at all,' and astounded to discover that her every visitor had an utterly different face. Finally, a 22-year-old girl was dazzled by the world's brightness and kept her eyes shut for two weeks. When at the end of that time she opened her eyes again, she did not recognize any objects, but 'the more she now directed her gaze upon everything about her, the more it could be seen how an expression of gratification and astonishment overspread her features; she repeatedly exclaimed: "O God! How beautiful!"'" (Annie Dillard, *Pilgrim at Tinker Creek* [New York: HarperCollins, 1990], pp. 34, 35, quoting Marius von Senden, *Space and Sight*).

It is right that the young woman should associate her new eyes with God. The deception that led to the Fall of humankind was visual. "So when the woman saw that the tree . . . was a delight to the eyes . . . she took of its fruit and ate; and she also gave some to her husband. . . . Then the eyes of both were opened, and they knew that they were naked" (Genesis 3:6, 7). Jesus noted the diminution of vision that resulted from sin by quoting Isaiah: "For this people's heart has grown dull, and their ears are hard of hearing, and they have shut their eyes; so that they might not look with their eyes, and listen with their ears, and understand with their heart and turn—and I would heal them" (Matthew 13:15).

Jesus came to restore our sight. He announced this at the beginning of His ministry by quoting Isaiah to His hometown congregation in Nazareth:

> God's Spirit is on me;
>> he's chosen me to preach the Message of good news to
>>> the poor,
> Sent me to announce pardon to prisoners and
>> recovery of sight to the blind,
> To set the burdened and battered free,
>> to announce, "This is God's year to act!" (Luke 4:18, 19,
>>> Message).

In that spirit, I want to tell you about the greatest Christmas gift that I ever received—eyes from my father.

Strabismus is the medical name for the condition of abnormal deviation or alignment of one eye in relation to another. It is caused by the lack of muscle coordination between the eyes, causing the eyes to point in different directions.

Strabismus is my condition. I was born with crossed eyes.

My mother took me to church for the first time. She was proud of this last child, born in her forty-fourth year and healthy after the death of an infant from a congenital heart defect 18 months before. I represented a risk taken in the hope for one more child to fill the house with laughter and love. I'm told that a teenage girl standing on the church sidewalk asked to look in the blanketed bundle and, ignoring the miracle that was me, said, "Oooh, something is wrong with his eyes."

This was the start of a lifetime of comments. My earliest memories are of my big brother Terry fighting other kids who made fun of my "weird eyes." "What's the matter with your eyes? Are you retarded or sumthin'?"

were a brace of grade school questions that I frequently struggled to answer through my intense desire to be accepted.

It is important for a lawyer to look people in their eyes. After years of having persons I am talking with glance over their shoulders to see who I am looking at when no one else is in my office, and having them withhold their handshake because they think I am greeting someone else beside them, I have to force myself to look up at people. It has made me wary of jury trials at which eye contact is a crucial part of persuasion.

There are strategies to compensate. For instance, in my frequent public speaking engagements I have learned to handle questioners who can't tell that I'm calling on them. "The woman in the back in the red suit, what is your question?" I'll ask. "The man in the blue and gold striped tie, what would you like to discuss?" They'll look around and then down at their attire before speaking up. It borders on the rude, but it works after I've pointed and nodded to no avail at their raised hands.

My spouse and friends tell me it doesn't matter, that the condition is noticeable only when I'm tired. All I know is that self-conscious or not, I have to talk to people to make a living and I have to resist the compulsion to avert my eyes in shame.

There is soft spot in my heart for Ulysses S. Grant, whose wife, Julia, had a form of strabismus. When he was elected president, Julia was very conscious of how the visible defect in her eyes would affect her image as first lady. She decided to undergo what was then a dangerous surgical procedure in an attempt to improve her appearance and reduce embarrassment to her husband. Grant learned of this. "Please don't do this for me. I like you just the way you are," he told her.

It is the reaction of others to my wandering eyes that is the problem, not what I can see through those eyes. Even in middle age I read and drive without glasses. My condition would be much worse if it wasn't for the Christmas gift of my sight. Most persons see binocularly, one image through both eyes. Strabismus can form a double image, one in each eye, and the brain suppresses the image of the diverting eye, causing amblyopia and leading to a vision loss in the nondominant eye. In serious cases such as mine, surgery can strengthen or weaken the muscles that regulate the movement of the eyeball. The eyes can be surgically realigned to restore single binocular vision, thus saving the sight in the nondominant eye. To be effective, the surgery must be done in early childhood.

There was no health insurance in 1957 when I needed the surgery. My father was a carpenter and building contractor who worked very hard for not much money. My eldest brother had been seriously injured in an accident requiring multiple hospitalizations. My sister had a mysterious paralyzing disease that stumped a series of expensive specialists. Then there were the expenses of the intense battle to save the life of the infant daughter. There were church school bills that my parents considered a necessity, and there was always a faithful tithe returned. There was simply no money to pay for the surgery that Dr. Culver, the ophthalmologist, said I needed to see in both eyes and improve my appearance.

Dr. Culver lived out of town on California's central coast. His home's driveway passed through a ravine that would flood in the winter, cutting off access for days. Learning of my father's vocation, Dr. Culver proposed a trade. If my father would build him a bridge, Dr. Culver would perform my surgery.

So my father built the bridge. This was a major undertaking; the ravine was deep with steep sides. Pilings had to be secured in the streambed to anchor the structure. Then a trestle was built up from the base. It took a month, a time of sacrifice for my whole family, since there was no other source of income for our household needs.

The surgery was done in December, the week before Christmas. I remember the strangeness of the hospital, coming to in complete darkness with my mother staying awake beside me each night, reading to me so I wouldn't pull off the bandages covering my eyes. There was the warm sawdust smell of my father when he would stop by on the way home from work and lay his stubbly cheek against mine. The ice cream the hospital served me was a cold sweet sensation in the dark. When I came home our fox terrier, Spot, gave me wet lavish licks of greeting as I squealed and fumbled to pet him.

The bandages came off Christmas eve to the wonders of the lighted tree and a red tricycle my father had refurbished and repainted. My father built a bridge so I could see it all. He built that bridge not for money or for achievement. He built that bridge for love of his child.

It may be that you reading this are challenged by the chasm of a misunderstanding that you can't correct; by a dividing difference that you cannot overcome; by an oppressive burden that leaves you vulnerable and ashamed; by a physical disability that walls you off from freedom and intimacy; by a sorrow that has slammed you to the floor without breath; by a thick, disorienting darkness that leaves you groping at nothing. If you never read another word I write beyond this day, stick with me now on this point. You are God's child. Your heavenly Father built a bridge for the love of you. It is anchored deep on the stout wooden legs of a manger in Bethlehem and the blood-stained crossties of Calvary and the pillars of heaven and in the secret recesses of your very heart. The Son of God Himself, love's pure light, placing His feet in our very human footprints with His hand raised to His Father above, holding on to what He could no longer see, became that bridge for us. He is the Christmas miracle, the complete package—the bridge that we cross, the eyes to see us through the crossing, and the strength to carry us across. He is Jesus Christ, and He is God's Everything.

The apostle John succinctly described the superstructure of this bridge: "This is how God showed his love for us: God sent his only Son into the world so we might live through him. This is the kind of love we are talking about—not that we once upon a time loved God, but that he loved us and sent his Son as a sacrifice to clear away our sins and the damage they've done to our relationship with God" (1 John 4:9, 10, Message).

When it is all said and done, knowing that my father loved me enough to build that bridge so I could see takes the sting out of that other stuff about my eyes. If you know you are really loved no matter what, you can endure anything and can move ahead in enlightened freedom. Much more than we can ask or think does our heavenly Father love you and me. If that truth registers in our heart, not just our head, it changes how we view everything. The apostle Paul prayed that every believer would receive this life-changing vision:

"I pray that the God of our Lord Jesus Christ, the Father of glory, may give you a spirit of wisdom and revelation as you come to know him, so that, *with the eyes of your heart enlightened,* you may know what is the hope to which he has called you, what are the riches of his glorious inheritance among the saints, and what is the immeasurable greatness of his power for us who believe, according to the working of his great power" (Ephesians 1:17-19).

It is the desire of God's heart that we see ourselves as we were created to be—His precious, beloved children.

TWENTY-ONE

Tell What You Know

"To tell what you know, and only what you know"
is a lesson of witness.

I attended camp meeting every summer as a boy. This was a special 10-day gathering of the members of my denomination in central California. There were meetings in big circus-style tents for people of all ages. It was a common practice to bring in, for the teenagers, speakers "who had tasted of the world" and were unsatisfied by what they found there. Thus we would hear from men and women who had rebelled against their parents and their religious upbringing, run away from home, joined a rock band, and partaken liberally of drugs, alcohol, and sex. None of these things satisfied them, they would tell us; only Jesus satisfies. Yes, they were done with what the world called "fun," and now they were serious about God.

We sat listening to the emotional pulls and tugs. It was confusing. Most of us were whole-wheat bread-eating, church school-educated, sheltered kids. The only wild oats we knew were growing on the hills above the campground. The most sinful thought that most of us had was whether the girl from Fresno or Visalia or wherever that we had just met would hold hands and write us after camp meeting was over. What were the youth ministers who solicited these testimonies really telling us? That to have a witness we would have to go out and raise some Cain? That stuff we had never thought about was really bad for us and now that we had heard about it, we shouldn't think about it anymore? That unless you had sunk to the depths of depravity you had nothing to talk about? The serpent can slither into Eden in a number of ways.

Some of the dumbest things I ever heard came out of these meetings. The Beatles were a Communist plot. Smoking cigarettes would permanently lower your IQ by a third in the first week. The fact that your palms didn't sweat after the third or fourth time you held hands with the same girl meant your metabolisms were synchronizing and this would lead to pregnancy. (There are legitimate issues to be raised about rock music, dating relationships, and substance abuse, but it is axiomatic that teaching morality by fear leads to bad morals.) On the other hand, there was nary a word about loneliness, acne, getting along with your parents, responsibility in dealing with the opposite sex, exercising discernment and taste in entertainment and recreation, and rarely a word about grace. I don't think anyone was really harmed by this, but the tragedy was that few of us were helped. Of course, we had fun talking and playing with each other and enjoying time with our families—that was where the real fun was, but who would admit it?

Fast-forward 30 years. I sit in a rocking chair leading a small group discussion on the book of Jeremiah. Across from me sits a nicely dressed older man. The question before the group is "What is the deepest truth you know that will hold even if everything else fails?" "That God loves me" is the answer most people give, with variations on the theme. He is last. He fidgets and twists his hands in his lap and says, "I don't know. I really have nothing to say. I've never gone through the things the rest of you have. I've had such an uneventful and good life that I think God must have some horrible death in store for me. I really have nothing to say."

I am incredulous. He has been a church member all his life. He has had material prosperity, but he was emotionally abused in childhood. His marriage failed. His children have not done well. He has stood by his religion through all of it only to think God will cause him great suffering in the end. And he has nothing to say? Are we speaking of faith or superstition here?

Tony Campolo tells the story of a Baptist pastor friend who was prevailed upon by a woman in his congregation to baptize her 7-year-old daughter. He didn't want to do it, because he didn't think that she'd had a genuine conversion by choice. It is the practice of the Baptists to baptize only believers. The woman was so insistent that he thought it best to give in.

It was the custom of this congregation for the baptismal candidate to give a personal testimony about his or her conversion at the midweek prayer service. The night came when this little girl was to tell how she came to believe in Jesus and share, in her own words, something about her Christian experience.

The little girl started by saying, "For years I wandered deep in sin . . ."

Snickers and giggles went up among the people in the small congregation. She was obviously repeating what she had heard other people say and trying to pass it off as her own. Campolo concludes, "When Pilate asked Jesus if He really was the King of the Jews, the Lord answered, 'Are you saying this on your own initiative, or did others tell you about me?' (John 18:34, NASB). That question needs to be asked of every one of us when we make professions of faith" (*Let Me Tell You a Story* [Nashville: Word, 2000], pp. 207, 208).

What does it mean to be a witness? It means to tell the facts as you know them to be true from personal observation. The basic instructions that an attorney tells a witness before testifying are "Listen to the question. Tell the truth. Answer the question you're asked and no more. If you don't know, say so. Don't speculate. Stay cool." To talk about something you know nothing about is big trouble on the witness stand. The witness who does this can be seriously discredited on cross-examination. To say that you saw what you didn't see is a serious enough offense to make it into the Ten Commandments.

Peter blustered a lot about God and life, and if you track him through the Gospels and the book of Acts, he really never got to finish a speech that he started. Late in his life, however, he seemed to get the hang of witness when he wrote to the churches in Asia: "Do not fear what they fear, and do not be intimidated, but in your hearts sanctify Christ as Lord. Always be ready to make your defense to anyone who demands from you an accounting for the hope that is in you, yet do it with gentleness and reverence. Keep your conscience clear, so that, when you are maligned, those who abuse you for your good conduct in Christ may be put to shame" (1 Peter 3:14-16).

The point is to answer the question that you are actually asked with your own answer, not someone else's. That answer shouldn't be some glib platitude. Share the actual reason for the hope that is within you. Reason tells us that this is about thinking more than feeling. Hope is a choice. Why did you make that choice? Why do you acknowledge Christ as your Savior and the Lord of your life?

Even if we aren't called from a life of sex, drugs, and rock and roll, or if words come hard to us, we still can have an answer. What gets us up in the morning? Who helps us see beyond the day? If the answer is God and we trust that answer, then we can say "Thank You." Gratitude is the testimony of those who trust. Gratitude is the natural response of those who trust. David thought this through: "What shall I return to the Lord for all his bounty to me? I will lift up the cup of salvation and call on the name of the Lord. . . . I will offer you a thanksgiving sacrifice and call on the name of the Lord. I will pay my vows to the Lord in the presence of all his people" (Psalm 116:12-18).

Gratitude is the attitude of grace received.

The answer must run deeper than words. Witness refers to what is seen and heard. Testimony is only a description of what was witnessed. Read 1 Peter 3:14-16 again. Peter speaks of Christ in the heart, of a way of life in Christ—living with honesty, courage, and gentleness because the source of life is assured. Francis of Assisi told his followers: "Preach the gospel at all times. Use words if necessary." True believers do not merely tell the story; they *are* the story. The essential witness is to live the life that God gives us in Christ—a life empowered by the resurrected Christ. If you are living in fear and intimidation, you are not living that life, "for God did not give us a spirit of cowardice, but rather a spirit of power and of love and of self-discipline" (2 Timothy 1:7). Vincent Van Gogh never flinched from truth in his art, and he recognized the truth of Christ in life. "Christ," he wrote a friend, "is more of an artist than the artists; he works in the living spirit and the living flesh; he makes men instead of statues" (*The Complete Letters,* B 9, III, 499).

We make a mistake when we dwell on just one event of "conversion." The recognition and acceptance of salvation for most people occurs over a period of time, maybe even their whole lifetime. Our story is written in our waking and sleeping, our doubts and the glimpses of truth that illumine us, our sprints and our stumbling.

This is illustrated by the life of Baruch, the secretary to the distinguished prophet Jeremiah. His was a position of honor with the most significant religious leader of his time and place. Jeremiah dictated a prophecy of destruction to Judah because of the apostasy of the people. Baruch wrote down the prophecy and read it aloud in the Jerusalem Temple. The government officials who heard the reading invited Baruch to meet with them privately for another reading. They found Jeremiah's words disturbing. They asked for the scroll and told Baruch to go to Jeremiah and go into hiding with him.

In a matter of hours Baruch's orderly, scholarly world was turned upside down. The officials went back to the royal palace and read the prophecy to King Jehoiakim. Jehudi, a royal minister, read the prophecy to the king. Every few paragraphs Jehoiakim would ask for the scroll, and he would cut off that portion with a penknife and throw it into the fire with contempt. The officials begged the king to stop, but he cut and burned the whole scroll. Then he ordered the arrest of Baruch and Jeremiah. The Lord hid the two men from view, but they were living the insecure existence of fugitives.

Jeremiah's response was to dictate the prophecy to Baruch again, only this time Jehoiakim's gruesome death was prophesied because of his defiance of the word of God. Baruch's great job and life had turned into a nightmare (Jeremiah 36). Baruch groaned out a prayer: "Woe is me! The Lord has added sorrow to my pain; I am weary with my groaning, and I find no rest" (Jeremiah 45:3).

Just as Van Gogh said, God was sculpting a man out of Baruch. God sent word to Baruch via Jeremiah: "I am going to break apart and tear up the whole land. I know you have sought greatness for yourself. Stop, because there is going to be disaster enough to go around for everyone. But you— *I will give you your life as a prize of war wherever you go"* (verses 4, 5, paraphrase).

This is it, you know—the heart of witness. Stuff happens. Good stuff and the disasters, wars, and fugitive flights of our existence. God gives us life wherever and whenever we go. We can blame God or we can thank God, but our life is a gift either way. Living the life that we are given in recognition of the gift—that is witness. The words of my favorite song rise in my soul at the thought:

> Blessed assurance, Jesus is mine!
> O, what a foretaste of glory divine!
> Heir of salvation, purchase of God,
> Born of His Spirit, washed in His blood.
>
> This is *my story,* this is *my song,*
> Praising *my Savior* all the day long;
> This is *my story,* this is *my song,*
> Praising *my Savior* all the day long.
>
> —Fanny J. Crosby

May the Lord Jesus Christ grant you your life as a prize of war wherever you may go. Your life is grace. This is your story. This is your song. This is your witness. This is what you talk about when they ask you about the hope that is within you.

TWENTY-TWO

Smoky Mountain Spring

A lawyer on a business trip glimpses the
majesty of God on a walk through the Georgia woods.

I attended a conference on the eastern slope of the Great Smoky Mountains in Georgia. The conference center is located on a low ridge that extends out into a lake that surrounds it on three sides. Beyond the lake and surrounding its valley are mountains rising in thickly forested phalanxes.

Arriving early, I grabbed my Bible and a bottle of water and headed into the woods. It was morning, and the clouds hung on the mountaintops. A grassy trail beckoned across the earthen dam at the head of the lake. On the other side was a gravel path through trees of every description—pines, maples, beeches, and oaks of various kinds breaking into leaf. There were bursts of white and pink dogwood, pink rhododendron, purple lilacs, blue columbine, and red star-shaped flowers whose name I do not know.

Nothing in my reading or imagination prepared this California boy for a Southern spring—positively nuclear in its energy. A hum sounded under and over everything. I listened for a long time, and insects alone did not explain this hum. It was part insect, part wind. But mostly I think it was an electrical charge from photosynthesis in overload. The spectrum of greens from light to dark overwhelmed me. Looking at a tree-lined hill there was like looking at a large box of crayons with nothing but shades of green. Birdcalls punctuated everything.

I entered these woods a very tired lawyer. The exhaustion had built for weeks. My job often finds me listening to what I don't want to hear and telling others what they don't want to hear. The difference between the Christ in my heart and the world of flesh around me is so dissonant that my prayer, as my journal will attest, is too frequently a pitiful begging for relief. But in the trees, at the midpoint of April, with the world giving exuberant birth around me, the weariness began to drain away, displaced by wonder.

There was a six-sided, peak-roofed shelter on the rocky point of the cliff above the lake. A plaque on a rock identified the place as a prayer garden in memory of a pastor who came there to pray. I sat on a bench overlooking the lake, the grounds of the conference center and the mountains rising in green glory to the clouds beyond. I had no words to pray. My silent seeking that brought me there was my supplication.

In my heart stirred an urging to read Psalm 36. I pulled out my Bible to see what was said there. It is a vision of David about a man who has ceased to be wise and do good, who flatters himself and compromises his course of action, failing to detect or reject the wrong. I can identify with this. My heart is "prone to wander, . . . prone to leave the God I love." Then came the words bearing a flood tide of grace and truth:

> Your love, O Lord, reaches to the heavens,
>> your faithfulness to the skies.
> Your righteousness is like the mighty mountains,
>> your justice like the great deep.
> O Lord, you preserve both man and beast.
>> How priceless is your unfailing love!
> Both high and low among men
>> find refuge in the shadow of your wings.
> They feast on the abundance of your house;
>> you give them drink from your river of delights.
> For with you is the fountain of life;
>> in your light we see light.
> Continue your love to those who know you,
>> your righteousness to the upright in heart
>> (Psalm 36:5-10, NIV).

Looking upon these ancient mountains and reading David's prayer, the Word was made flesh before my eyes and in my heart. I stood and walked on, filled with praise and thanksgiving, my sole request to know and be known in a deeper way by my Lord, Creator, and Redeemer.

Springs dripped from shale cliffs seamed with anthracite coal. Little waterfalls tumbled down and across the trail into the lake. Years of work in a law firm that practices water law has taught me about such things. The rain and the snow fall on the mountains and seep down into the earth and rocky crevices. The water is caught and held in subterranean reservoirs formed by dams of hard rock. When these pools are filled to overflowing, the earth can no longer contain their volume, and the resulting pressure causes the waters to "spring" out of the earth.

So it is with our hearts. The rain and the snow of experience fall upon our heads perhaps in the cold winter of our existence when the trees of our life are stripped of leaves. This moisture, perhaps unbearable at the time, seeps down into the crevices of our soul, where it forms silent pools. When enough of it builds, in the springtime of our new life, it bubbles out of us again, only this time as life-giving water for the growth of our new experience. By such things does God renew you and me.

I came upon a clear-water pond in the woods. I sat beside it and watched large bass rise and bask in the midday sun. All was well in my soul when I left the forest. From childhood on the central coast of California I have needed time in the solitude of the wild at least once a month, or else I become diseased and fragmented. I think that times like this—in the mountains, beside a stream, in a garden, or at the ocean—are needed by everyone to be complete. How can we learn what God is like or the divine intention for us unless we listen to Him express Himself from the heart of the earth. Walt Whitman wrote this very thought:

> There was a child went forth every day,
> And the first object he look'd upon, that object he became,
> And that object became part of him for the day or a certain part of
>   the day,
> Or for many years . . .
> The early lilacs became part of this child,
> And grass and white and red morning-glories,
>   and white and red clover, and the song of the phoebe bird,
> And the Third-month lambs and the sow's pink-faint litter,
>   and the mare's foal and the cow's calf,
> And the noisy brood of the barnyard or by the mire of the pond-side,
> And the fish suspending themselves so curiously below there,
>   and the beautiful curious liquid,

And the water-plants with their graceful flat heads, all became part
of him.

May the grace of God's good spring be yours this week and always.
May you be filled with the resurrected and living glory of Jesus Christ—
for this is the ultimate renewal and the eternal spring.

TWENTY-THREE

The Seduction of Shelter

The very thing that we turn to for survival can draw the life from us. Faith forgoes security and instant gratification.

The Southwestern deserts of the United States are sun-bleached and wind-scoured. Nothing grows tall there except occasional cotton-wood trees around springs and the seasonal streams. Yet people came into this land. Native Americans adapted to the desert and even learned to farm it. Later, European settlers built their adobe-and-stone dwellings to shelter against the sun and wind. Shade was hard to come by, and they longed for the trees of their homelands. They tried many varieties that did not survive in the alkaline soils and blast-furnace climate. One tree that did make it was the tamarisk, a transplant from the Middle East with blue-green scalelike leaves and pink blossoms. Here is a description of these trees by the great American author Willa Cather, from her book *Death Comes for the Archbishop* (New York: Vintage Classics, 1990):

"On the south, against the earth wall, was the one row of trees they had found growing there when they first came—old, old tamarisks, with twisted trunks. They had been so neglected, left to fight for life in such hard, sun-baked, burro-trodden ground, that their trunks had the hardness of cypress. They looked, indeed, like very old posts, well seasoned and polished by time, miraculously endowed with the power to burst into delicate foliage and flowers, to cover themselves with long brooms of lavender-pink blossom.

"Father Joseph had come to love the tamarisk above all trees. It had been the companion of his wanderings. All along his way through the deserts of New Mexico and Arizona, wherever he had come upon a Mexican homestead, out of the sun-baked earth, against the sun-baked adobe walls, the tamarisk waved its feathery plumes of bluish green. The family burro was tied to its trunk, the chickens scratched under it, the dogs slept in its shade, the washing was hung on its branches. Father Latour had often remarked that this tree seemed especially designed in shape and colour for the adobe village. The sprays of bloom which adorn it are merely another shade of the red earth walls, and its fibrous trunk is full of gold and lavender tints. Father Joseph respected the bishop's eye for such things, but himself he loved it merely because it was the tree of the people, and was like one of the family in every Mexican household" (pp. 201, 202).

In seeking some color, shade, and a break against the wind, the settlers traded off something else. The tamarisk sends its roots deep into the ground and sucks up all available water, killing off all other vegetation in its vicinity. Tamarisk trees have forced out native plant species and have taken over great swatches of desert terrain. They are considered a nuisance, and the Bureau of Land Management sponsors programs to eradicate them.

Do we make trade-offs like this? Desperate for shelter in a dry, hot place, and eager for some color in a drab, weary existence, do we seek it from things that eventually drain our life away—a relationship, a possession, a fantasy, an ambition?

The children of Israel lived encircled by enemies, dependent on God for provision and protection in a vulnerable existence. The nations around them had kings with visible stable governments and standing armies. When eyes turn from heaven to the horizons, comparisons begin to erode the spirit of grace that sustained them.

"Give us a king to govern us," they shouted to their prophet and judge, Samuel.

Samuel was displeased and prayed to the Lord about this rejection. "They haven't rejected you," God answered. "They have rejected Me as their king and My ways as their ways. They have forgotten how I delivered them from captivity in Egypt and serve other gods. They are only doing to you, Samuel, what they've done to Me. So listen to their request, but tell them what having a king will be like for them."

Samuel told them, "A king will draft your sons to fight his wars and tax your income and property to fund his armies and lifestyle. He will take your daughters to work in his palaces and the best of your harvest to feed himself. Your standard of living will suffer. You are giving up the freedom you have in God to be the slaves of an expensive, oppressive monarchy."

"We don't care," the people told Samuel. "We are determined to have a king so that we may be like other nations and our king can tell us what to do and fight our battles for us."

The gracious Lord told Samuel, "Let them have what they want" (see 1 Samuel 8:4-22).

They received their king, became like everyone else, and centuries of tyranny and despotism followed. Sure there was a David, a Solomon, and a Hezekiah. There was also a bipolar, narcissistic Saul willing to drive his hungry, tired men on a fool's errand after Philistines and to sacrifice his son on a whim. There were thugs and idolaters and psychopaths. The history beyond the demand for a king to rule over them was a root spiraling down deep into darkness, sucking away the life-giving water of grace from the Hebrews.

It is human to want protection from a harsh environment, to desire encircling arms in our loneliness, to seek security in an uncertain world. It is God's covenant of grace to cover and provide for us if we will only wait and focus on Him. That covenant was described by Moses in his valedictory address recorded in Deuteronomy. He ended with these words that always move me:

"See, I have set before you today life and prosperity, death and adversity. If you obey the commandments of the Lord your God that I am commanding you today, by loving the Lord your God, walking in his ways, and observing his commandments, decrees, and ordinances, then you shall live and become numerous, and the Lord your God will bless you in the land that you are entering to possess. But if your heart turns away and you do not hear, but are led astray to bow down to other gods and serve them, I declare to you today that you shall perish; you shall not live long in the land that you are crossing the Jordan to enter and possess. I call heaven and earth to witness against you today that I have set before you life and death, blessings and curses. Choose life so that you and your descendants may live, loving the Lord your God, obeying him, and holding fast to him; for that means life to you and length of days, so that you may live in the land that the Lord swore to give to your ancestors, to Abraham, to Isaac, and to Jacob" (Deuteronomy 30:15-20).

To choose life always means to choose our Creator and Redeemer, even in the seduction of the immediate demands of loneliness, doubt, anger, fear, hunger, frustration, pain, and grief. When we are in the desert of those thoughts and feelings, how we long for some shade and cheering blossoms. We need some understanding that there will be another side of this crossing. If we turn aside to take our comfort and our hope when and as we can grab them from whomever and wherever, we are choosing death. Our life will drain away in the process. There is one Creator, one Lord, one Redeemer of us all, and life and love and regeneration are the unique gifts of the one who made us and knows us best. David realized this when he wrote the first passage of Scripture that I ever memorized and the one that I hope that my heart sings with the last breath that I ever take on this earth:

> The Lord is my shepherd, I shall not want.
>   He makes me lie down in green pastures;
> he leads me beside still waters;
>   he restores my soul.
> He leads me in right paths
>   for his name's sake.
>
> Even though I walk through the darkest valley,
>   I fear no evil;
> for you are with me;
>   your rod and your staff—
>   they comfort me.
>
> You prepare a table for me
>   in the presence of my enemies;
> you anoint my head with oil;
>   my cup overflows.
>
> Surely goodness and mercy shall follow me
>   all the days of my life,
> and I shall dwell in the house of the Lord
>   my whole life long (Psalm 23).

These words were not written for the back page of the funeral programs, where we most often read them. Child of grace, do you believe these words about your living God? If so, do not settle for less. Do not plant for immediate gratification what will grow demanding and kill off the life of your soul. Do not seek a "king" in the illusion of security and conformity that will demand of you everything but cannot sustain the promise, eventually breaking the promise and your heart along with it. You were created by a God who loves you. You were redeemed by a God who cares for you. You have a home with a God who will never move away from you. You, as God's child, deserve nothing less. Please do not settle for less.

TWENTY-FOUR

The Referral

*A lawyer and client meeting over criminal charges turns into a
moment of redeeming grace.*

A local business executive sent me a client. He asked me to see
her. "She's in trouble and can use a lawyer" was all he said. She
came to see me on a stormy Tuesday afternoon—a waif in a wet, over-
sized raincoat.

Her head hung down. Her responses to my initial questions were
monosyllabic. She was twentysomething and scared, obviously depressed.
The scenario developed slowly and painfully.

"So why do you need to see an attorney?"

"I stole money at work."

"Where do you work?"

"A bank."

"Oh. What do you do at the bank?"

"I'm an assistant manager."

"How much did you take?"

"The audit found $10,000."

"What happened then?"

"Bank security talked to me. I've been suspended."

"Did they tell you what they are going to do next?"

"They told me they would contact me."

"I'm sure they will."

She kept her head down as she answered. There was no eye contact.

"Is that all the money you took?"

Silence.

"Anything you tell me here is privileged. I can help you only if you
are honest with me. Are the auditors going to find more money missing?"

"Yes."

"How much more?"

"They could find $40,000."

"Believe me, the bank is not going to overlook $40,000. Why did you take it?"

"I was angry."

"Angry at whom?"

"Pretty much everyone. Nobody cared at work. Nobody listened at home. So I just took it."

"Do you still have the money?"

She shook her head no.

"What did you do with it?"

"I spent it on stuff."

"What stuff?"

"A car, clothes, paying off credit cards."

"What does your husband have to do with this?"

"He doesn't know and he couldn't care less." Tears begin to run out of her large brown eyes. With her head tilted down, they rolled off her nose and onto the raincoat.

"Hey," I asked, "what's really going on with you?" I pushed a box of Kleenex across the desk to her.

Her story began to dribble out in gasped pauses between sobs.

She had been released from a mental hospital that morning. She had been admitted after a suicide attempt.

There was posttraumatic stress from a sexual assault. Her parents and husband blamed her for the rape. She had suffered a miscarriage. Her marriage was breaking up. She was mad and broken and ashamed. Taking the money was an act of raging revenge and self-destruction.

After a while her voice just trailed off and she stared at the carpet.

"OK," I said. "You do need an attorney, but it needs to be a criminal defense specialist. The bank's money is federally insured. The FBI is going to be involved. I am a business lawyer, and I don't handle criminal cases. I'll need to refer you to another attorney. OK?"

She shrugged.

"Your best chance is to cut a deal with the prosecutor based on first offense and restitution. The criminal attorneys know the prosecutors and can talk to them. I'll call one right now."

I looked up a number and reached for the phone. A Bible verse came into my mind: "I have no silver or gold, but what I have I give you" (Acts 3:6).

I tried to shove the words out of my mind, but the Holy Spirit was insistent. I saw with clarity what the verse meant. The "silver and gold" was legal representation. What I had to offer was God. I prayed silently in my heart. "Father, I can't represent this woman, but I know You. Will You help her?"

Replacing the phone receiver, I asked, "Do you have any kind of spiritual background?"

"I went to church when I was a little girl."

"Look, I can't represent you, but I want to tell you about someone who can help you. You've done something here that I haven't done, but I've done things that hurt people and made me feel really bad. But I found that God loves me and forgives me, and no matter what the consequences of what I've done He'll meet them with me. Is it OK with you to talk about this for a while?"

She looked up at me for the first time and nodded yes.

"You will likely go to jail. The FBI may come and arrest you at your home and take you away in handcuffs in front of your neighbors. But you know what? God promises that He'll be there with you every step of the way. He'll go to jail with you. He'll go to court with you. Nothing can separate you from His love. Nothing!"

I reached in the bookcase behind my desk and pulled out a Bible. "There was man named David," I told her. "The Bible talks a lot about him and contains many of his own prayers and songs. His boss, the king, turned on him, and he was a fugitive on the run, hiding in a cave. He prayed this prayer:

> With my voice I cry to the Lord;
> > with my voice I make supplication to the Lord.
> I pour out my complaint before him;
> > I tell my trouble before him.
> When my spirit is faint,
> > you know my way.
>
> In the path where I walk

they have hidden a trap for me.
Look on my right hand and see—
    there is no one who takes notice of me;
no refuge remains to me;
    no one cares for me.

I cry to you, O Lord;
    I say, "You are my refuge,
    my portion in the land of the living."
Give heed to my cry,
    for I am brought very low.

Save me from my persecutors,
    for they are too strong for me.
Bring me out of prison,
    so that I may give thanks to your name.
The righteous will surround me,
    for you will deal bountifully with me (Psalm 142).

"Is this how you feel right now? Trapped, and thinking that no one cares whether you live or die? God cares. He will hold your hand through this, through the shame and the punishment. On the other side is a whole family of His children that will love and support you. That's what David meant when he said, 'After I get out of this prison the righteous will surround me, for You [that's God] will deal bountifully with me [that's you].'

"You know how He does this?" I asked her.

"No."

"God's Son, Jesus Christ, came to earth and became a human, lived and died as one of us, and went through everything we go through. The authorities condemned Jesus to die, and when He died He died for the sins of every other human, including you and me, so that through Him we are forgiven and can live with Him forever in heaven. Jesus described it this way: 'For God so loved the world that he gave his only Son, so that everyone who believes in him may not perish but may have eternal life' [John 3:16].

"Once we know, really know in here [I pointed to my heart] that we are loved and we will live forever in that love, we can face anything, even death.

"Jesus' follower Paul said that God would not hold back anything to save us, even His Son. Jesus willingly took all the condemnation dumped on us and absorbed it. No matter what we have done, no matter what is done to us, Jesus will not stop loving us or leave us. Here is what Paul wrote: 'Who will separate us from the love of Christ? Will hardship, or distress, or persecution, or famine, or nakedness, or peril, or sword? . . . No, in all these things we are more than conquerors through him who loved us.' Now listen closely, 'For I am convinced that neither death, nor life, nor angels, nor rulers, nor things present, nor things to come, nor powers, nor height, nor depth, nor anything else in all creation, will be able to separate us from the love of God in Christ Jesus our Lord' [Romans 8:35-39]."

I closed the Bible and asked her, "Do you understand what I am telling you? Do you believe this?"

The tears flowed down her cheeks as she nodded yes.

We sat in silence. Outside my window, traffic sloshed through the intersection of Sixth and Main and the wind whipped the leaves of the lemon gum trees. Inside, our hearts could sense the breath of heaven exhaling in release.

I picked up the phone again to arrange for defense counsel. She reached across my desk and picked up my Bible. She leafed through it as I talked to the other attorney.

When I was through with the call I asked her, "Would you like to have that Bible?"

She was surprised. "You would give me your Bible?"

"Yes, if you want it."

"I do. Thank you."

"Here, let me write out where you can find the verses that I read to you. Please go home and read them again for yourself."

We went over the information for the appointment with her counsel. We stood. I gave her a hug. "Everything I told you today is true," I said.

"I know that," she said.

Months later she sent me a card with this message:

"I want to thank you for what you have done for me. . . . I have been doing better these past days. I met with the FBI. My lawyer was there. He is a great lawyer. But like you said, lawyers, judges, and people could not really help. It's just praying to God, who could help, and to believe in Him. He said during our times of trial is when He carries us. God bless you."

She went on through a fine and imprisonment to a new life with a restored marriage and a baby.

If I live to be 100 and through eternity, I will never tire of the thrill of glimpsing God at work, pouring oil on wounds, breathing life into tired bodies, cleansing hearts broken and soiled beyond recognition. "Come to Me," He whispers. "Come to Me, tired, oppressed soul, thrashing about without peace or hope, and I'll take over and give you rest." This is a standing invitation. Accepting it is everything.

TWENTY-FIVE

The Temptation to Fix It

*Our yielding to the temptation to fix it
is often the greatest hindrance to grace.*

Generations of my family from Denmark to Minnesota to California built houses, barns, churches, and dormitories. They could conceive these structures, design them, build them, and repair them. That is how my father made his living, and my grandfather before him, and his father, and on back. The profit of sweat, 16-penny nails in 2" x 4" Douglas fir studs, sand and mortar, plaster and paint paid for all of us to go to college—brothers and sister and cousins. We did not return to building. A few in my generation still had the talent in their hands for the occasional home improvement project. I do not share the birthright, and I feel the loss keenly.

I worked for my father in the summers in my teen years. It was unskilled labor: footings dug, subfloor nailed, blocks and lumber carried. Father tolerated me there. There was no magic of corners, windows, wiring, and plumbing in my hands. No secrets of wood grain and square footage, angle and finish in my soul. My back was strong, but my fingers bumbled and my mind wandered away from the task at hand.

When my wife and I returned from law school one summer to visit Mom and Dad, I deluded myself into thinking that marriage and education might have changed me. I didn't want to be some egghead intellectual. I wanted to do manly things—fix something with brawn and savvy.

The back steps of the farmhouse needed straightening and renailing. I could do this. With hammer and nails I approached my self-appointed task on a Friday afternoon. But first I would straighten up the posts with the sledgehammer. Just a few taps on this side and that. And then the whole back steps—banister, landing, and all—fell away from the house and onto the lawn, leaving the back porch high and inaccessible except with a ladder.

Father took the sledgehammer from my hand. "Oh, Kent," he said. "Don't do that." Then he laughed until tears came, and so did I.

We are tempted to fix things—buildings, problems, and maybe people. We are tempted to fix them beyond our competence and, worse, beyond our calling. Peter, for instance:

- tried to talk Jesus out of His destiny of suffering (Matthew 16:21-23);
- told the tax collectors that Jesus paid the Temple tax without asking Jesus (Matthew 17:24-27);
- made a pitch to be useful in the presence of the transfigured Christ (Mark 9:2-8);
- hacked off the ear of the high priest's servant during the arrest of Jesus (John 18:10, 11);
- insisted on casting lots for the successor to Judas while somewhere else God was preparing a Saul to be Paul (Acts 1:15-26); and
- tried to keep the peace with legalists in Galatia by refusing to eat with Gentile brothers and sisters to the disgust of Paul (Galatians 2:11-14).

I'm like Peter—shoot first and ask questions afterward. The prayer of "crop failure"—"O Lord, do not let these seeds of disaster that I have sown in my impatience and anger grow into plants"—is a frequent prayer of mine.

Jesus, on the other hand, knew Peter was going to betray Him and was going to suffer mightily for it. He did not give Peter three points and a poem to remember to avoid the failure. He didn't tell Peter, "Listen, you're going to go into the courtyard of the high priest's house tonight and they're going to ask you about Me. Say a prayer, and stand tall and witness." Or "Stay out of the high priest's house tonight or you'll blow your testimony."

This would have been good advice. But Jesus didn't come to give good advice. He did not come to "fix" us to be better. He came to transform us into an entirely new life—His life.

Jesus prayed for Peter. "Simon, Simon, listen! Satan has demanded to sift all of you like wheat, but I have prayed for you that your own faith may not fail; and you, when once you have turned back, strengthen your brothers" (Luke 22:31, 32). Jesus took Peter to the hands of His Father, who could transform Peter, not just fix him. "O what peace we often forfeit, O what needless pain we bear, all because we do not carry everything to God in prayer."

"Fixing it" is a temptation to resist. By fixing it, I mean forcing the issue, running ahead without asking why or where.

Instead of fixing it, we are called to yield to the enduring, insistent love that is greater than us, the grace of God that molds and shapes us in the inexorable power of eternity, the way a river forms a valley, the way a mother holds her infant firm and close before sleep.

Scripture describes some awful "fixes" by people wanting to push God's agenda. Consider these examples: Abraham and Hagar; Rebekah and Jacob tricking Isaac; Moses striking the rock in anger; Job's friends; Saul not waiting for Samuel to make the sacrifice; Uzzah trying to steady the ark; Caiaphas taking the step he thought necessary to preserve the nation; Saul killing Christians. There is some thought that Judas's betrayal of Jesus was a plan to force a confrontation leading to Jesus' triumphant proclamation as the Messiah.

Sometimes the fix results from an unthinking motivation to do something because of curiosity, self-consciousness, or fear.

Consider Martha in Luke 10:38-42. "I'm doing what needs to be done," she tells Jesus, "and don't You care that my sister Mary is lounging around and not helping me?" Jesus replies, "Why do you consider your Type A, workaholic, 'got-to-fix-it-right-now' personality a blessing? Mary has chosen to listen, and what she hears is going to stick with her, unlike your dinner, which, when it's eaten, will be gone." Did you ever wonder if home entertaining guru Martha Stewart's mother had a divine premonition when she picked the name?

The Christian nature writer Annie Dillard described a horrific fix that resulted from an out-of-control human urge to examine and "to have and to hold":

"Once, when I was 10 or 11 years old, my friend Judy brought in a polyphemus moth cocoon. It was January; there were doily snowflakes taped to the classroom panes. The teacher kept the cocoon in her desk all morning and brought it out when we were getting restless before recess. In a book we found what the adult moth would look like; it would be beautiful. With a wingspread of up to six inches, the polyphemus is one of the few huge American silk moths, much larger than, say, a giant or tiger swallowtail butterfly. The moth's enormous wings are velveted in a rich, warm brown and edged in bands of blue and pink delicate as a watercolor wash. A startling 'eyespot,' immense, and deep blue melding to an almost translucent yellow, luxuriates in the center of each hind wing. The effect is one of a masculine splendor foreign to the butterflies, a fragility unfurled to strength. The polyphemus moth in the picture looked like a mighty wraith, a beating essence of the hardwood forest, alien skinned and brown, with spread, blind eyes. This was the giant moth packed in the faded cocoon. We closed the book and turned to the cocoon. It was an oak leaf sewn into a plump oval bundle. Judy had found it loose in a pile of frozen leaves.

"We passed the cocoon around; it was heavy. As we held it in our hands, the creature within warmed and squirmed. We were delighted, and wrapped it tighter in our fists. The pupa began to jerk violently, in heart-stopping knocks. Who's there? I can still feel those thumps, urgent through a muffling of spun silk and leaf, urgent through the swaddling of many years, against the curve of my palm. We kept passing it around. When it came to me again it was as hot as a bun; it jumped half out of my hand. The teacher intervened. She put it, still heaving and banging, in the ubiquitous mason jar.

"It was coming. There was no stopping it now, January or not. One end of the cocoon dampened and gradually frayed in a furious battle. The whole cocoon twisted and slapped around in the bottom of the jar. The teacher fades, the classmates fade, I fade: I don't remember anything but that thing's struggle to be a moth or die trying. It emerged at last, a sodden crumple. It was a male; his long antennae were thickly plumed, as wide as his fat abdomen. His body was very thick, over an inch long, and deeply furred. A gray, furlike plush covered his head; a long, tan furlike hair hung from his wide thorax over his brown-furred, segmented abdomen. His multijointed legs, pale and powerful, were shaggy as a bear's. He stood still, but he breathed.

"He couldn't spread his wings. There was no room. The chemical that coated his wings like varnish, stiffening them permanently, dried, and hardened his wings as they were. He was a monster in a mason jar. Those huge wings stuck on his back in a torture of random pleats and folds, wrinkled as a dirty tissue, rigid as leather. They made a single nightmare clump still wracked with useless, frantic convulsions.

"The next thing that I remember, it was recess. The school was in Shadyside, a busy residential part of Pittsburgh. Everyone was playing dodgeball in the fenced playground or racing around the concrete schoolyard by the swings. Next to the playground a long delivery drive sloped downhill to the sidewalk and street. Someone—it must have been the teacher—had let the moth out. I was standing in the driveway, alone, stock-still, but shivering. Someone had given the polyphemus moth his freedom, and he was walking away.

"He heaved himself down the asphalt driveway by infinite degrees, unwavering. His hideous crumpled wings lay glued and tucked on his back, perfectly still now, like a collapsed tent. The bell rang twice; I had to go. The moth was receding down the driveway, dragging on. I went; I ran inside. The polyphemus moth is still crawling down the driveway, crawling down the driveway hunched, crawling down the driveway on six furred feet, forever" (Annie Dillard, *Pilgrim at Tinker Creek* [New York: HarperCollins, 1990], pp. 62-64).

Have you ever been forced to grow before your time, taken from the place where God put you, warmed by well-meaning but unthinking hands, placed on display, only to find yourself in a space too small and your wings glued shut? Have you ever done this to someone? One of the most dangerously misunderstood clichés in Christianity is "God has no other hands but ours." As a call to obedient service it is wonderful. As a license to "fix," it can be the first sentence of a horror story.

Paul writes the truth: "Let your gentleness be known to everyone. The Lord is near. Do not worry about anything, but in everything by prayer and supplication with thanksgiving let your requests be made known to God" (Philippians 4:5, 6).

Here is a poem by the Indian poet Rabindranath Tagore that beautifully conveys the idea:

> No, it is not yours to open buds into blossom.
> Shake the bud, strike it,
> it is beyond your power to make it blossom.
> Your touch soils it.
> You tear its petals to pieces
> and strew them in the dust,
> But no colors appear and no perfume.
> Oh, it is not for you to open the bud into blossom.
> He who can open the bud does it so simply.
> He gives it a glance and the life sap stirs through its veins.

At his breath the flower spreads its wings
and flutters in the wind.
Colors flash out like heart longings,
the perfume betrays a sweet secret.
He who can open the bud does it so simply.

I cannot be trusted with a sledgehammer and a 4" x 4" in my back-yard. The Lord of the universe, capable of stopping the sun with His bare hand and more, can be trusted to open a rosebud to full beauty on time. In the middle of the raw, sensitive inflammation that is your soul, you can trust Him to create a clean heart and renew a right spirit within you (Psalm 51:10). "Not by might, nor by power, but by my spirit, says the Lord of hosts" (Zechariah 4:6).

"He who can open the bud does it so simply." He who can open a heart can do it so simply. Just say yes.

TWENTY-SIX

The Owls

Two brothers on a moonlit walk are treated to a revelation
of the Creator's glory and grace through an encounter
with two great horned owls.

The final grounds of holy Fellowship are in God. Lives immersed and drowned in God are drowned in love, and know one another in Him, and know one another in love. God is the medium, the matrix, the focus, the solvent. As Meister Eckhart suggests, he who is wholly surrounded by God, enveloped by God, clothed with God, glowing in selfless love toward Him—such a man no one can touch except he touch God also. Such lives have a common meeting point; they live in a common joyous enslavement. They go back into a single Center where they are at home with Him and with one another. It is as if every soul had a final base, and that final base of every soul is one single Holy Ground, shared in by all. Persons in the Fellowship are related to one another by Him, as all mountains go down into the same earth. They get at one another through Him. He is actively moving in all, coordinating those who are pliant to His will and suffusing them all with His glory and His joy" (Thomas R. Kelly, *A Testament of Devotion* [San Francisco: Harper San Francisco, 1992], p. 56).

The October moon climbs the sky in full, golden glory. It pulls the tide of my heart over the whitewashed adobe wall of the retreat center. I resist that tug, earthbound by the material. My pen is missing.

It isn't just any pen. It is a $70 gold-plated Sheaffer classic fountain pen, my favorite. I love its rasp as it pushes words across the pages. Words are a gift, writing them is work, and the sound and heft of this pen remind me of both.

There is some guilt associated with this pen. I bought it on sale for $45 (bargains are in the deluded mind of the purchaser). It took mechanically challenged me two months of ink-spattered failure to learn how to place the cartridge correctly. I put it away for weeks until I happened to read the instructions on the back of the cartridge package and got the idea.

Tonight, when I went to meet with the retreat leader, I took my journal, my pocket New Testament, my Bible, and in my jacket pocket, the pen. When I returned to my room, opened up my journal, and reached for the pen, it wasn't there.

I looked around. The pen wasn't with my other stuff. "I must not have zipped my pocket." I tried to write with a $2.49 Pilot Varsity fountain pen (best writing and most reliable pen I've ever used). The thought of the missing pen would not let me rest.

So I am retracing my steps. At some point I leave the walk and cross the lawn. I see no gleam of gold in the moonlight. The retreat leader crosses the walk ahead of me. I pick up my head and quicken my step around the corner and out of sight. This is a man who once spent five months in prayer in a cave in Spain eating nothing but potatoes and water. He probably thinks that a 79-cent Bic ballpoint will do, and he's right.

The pen isn't in the empty conference room. Turning out the light, I step outside. To my left, in the dappled shadows of the porch, sits my brother Terry. We exchange nods. It is the third evening of a five-day silent retreat. Terry and I haven't exchanged a word for two days and three nights.

He sees me slowly zigzag across the lawn. "Did you lose something?" he calls out.

"Yeah, my pen. It's my favorite."

"The gold one?" he asks.

I say yes, knowing that he means my $5 Pentel roller ball (I am a pen junkie) that he borrowed on the first night. I don't correct him, because he probably won't approve of a $70 pen either.

I am across the first square of lawn before I realize that Terry is behind me and also looking.

The moon is higher, flooding light over us. Down the ridgeline, across the valley, I see the tallest hill that interested me during the day. It looks like it has antennae on top. My heart longs to wander beyond the walls, to explore the hills in the night.

I glance back at Terry, thinking, *My brother really loves me. He's restless tonight, and I'd love to do something special with him.*

But I don't want to break his silence, and I move ahead of him continuing the search. I wait for Terry to catch up to me in the rose garden, thinking I should get back to my prayer and the journal. The Spirit speaks to my heart: "The pen is gone for a reason. You came out here for more than a pen. Terry is waiting for something. Ask him."

I whisper to my brother, "Are you up for something silent but crazy?"

He looks at me quizzically. "Sure."

I gesture at his legs clad in shorts. "Are you warm enough?"

"Let me put on my long pants."

"Knock on my door when you're ready," I tell him.

Terry is a hospital executive. I am an attorney. Seven years separate us in age. We have different personalities and paths for our life, but the riches encountered on our journey with Christ are a shared bounty. I love my big brother with all my heart. He would be surprised to know that his name is the one most frequently found in the journals that I've kept for the past 12 years.

I open my door when I hear his door open, and we walk into the night without a word.

We cross the highway and start up the steep grassy slope beyond. Leaning into the hill, I push off the soft clods of a firebreak for traction. Terry follows a few steps behind. I suck air deep into my lungs to regulate my panting. Terry does the same. Stopping to rest, I think that we are both a lot older than the last time we climbed a hill together.

Our shadows against the illuminated ground are the difference of night and day.

We take a right on the ridge and walk down a saddle on a hard dirt road. Below we can hear engines accelerate, squealing tires, sirens, and an occasional indistinct voice.

When we ascend the hill it turns out to be a big knoll, commanding a view of what must be the ocean, dark and flat to the south; the blackness of the Camp Pendleton Marine base to the west; mesas and ravines in broken patterns to the east; and mountains on guard to the north—360 degrees of horizon. The antennae turn out to be two spindly old yucca plants stretching out of a patch of prickly pear. We stand in silence taking it in, Terry a bit higher on the slope than I.

Something flutters in front of me. A bat, I think, or a nighthawk. It is gone, and then there it is again—a moving shadow crossing the moonlit landscape. There are two of whatever they are.

Terry follows the line of my pointing finger and also sees the movement coming straight at us. Over our heads in swift smooth flight are two great horned owls. They swoop past us with flashes of golden eyes and translucent feathers. They settle on the yucca above us, one over the other, the big one on top, in the same positions that Terry and I stand on the hill. No more than 30 feet separate us.

Terry and I turn carefully in unison to watch. I am afraid that any movement will break the spell.

Silhouetted against the eastern sky, the owls begin to call to each other in deep, thrilling tones—*who-o-o, who, who, who-o-o*—back and forth at intervals, a conversation.

"O God," I pray in my soul, "this is amazing grace. Thank You for calling us here. Thank You for this brother of mine." My mouth is parted in wonder. All my thought, feeling, and physical being converge in focus. The moon shines down. It is perfect.

Unhurriedly the owls unfold their tremendous wings and take flight, one after the other, rising in slow swirling flames of gold, bronze, and copper ignited by the moon. They spiral up above us, coming together, then moving apart, then coming together again, exchanging calls in a dance of joy for the moon, the stars, and the night air that floats them in freedom between the earth and heaven—a reverent and wild expression of praise for the God who made us all. Then, as one, these night visitors return to their hunt over the fields, gliding away from our view.

Our world remains hushed for a long moment of benediction. I whisper to Terry, "That is one of the most wonderful things I've ever seen."

"Pure gift," he says.

He walks down to me, puts his arm around me, and kisses my forehead. He squeezes me hard. I squeeze back. We hold each other for a while, brothers by blood and in spirit, called to this time and place to witness the delight of God.

We start back, walking side by side with ease, downhill, around corners, back to the retreat center. Only one thing more is said. I whisper to Terry, "A psalm says that the moon is a faithful witness."

He murmurs "Mmm" in response.

That psalm is the first place in Scripture that God is called "Father." In it God speaks through David this message:

"He shall cry to me, 'You are my Father, my God, and the Rock of my salvation! . . .' Forever I will keep my steadfast love for him, and my covenant with him will stand firm . . . I will not remove from him my steadfast love, or be false to my faithfulness. . . . [His line] shall be established forever like the moon, an enduring witness in the skies" (Psalm 89:26-37).

Two brothers stand side by side on a moonlit hilltop in silent communion, naked in soul before God as they were the day their mother bore them into the world. The golden pen is forgotten. For the deepest secrets of God there are no words.

TWENTY-SEVEN

The Algorithm of Endurance

Often suffering seems to have no point, but our Creator can use even the worst of pain to do a work of transforming grace.

The apostle Paul wrote the Romans:

"Therefore, since we are justified by faith, we have peace with God through our Lord Jesus Christ, through whom we have obtained access to this grace in which we stand; and we boast in our hope of sharing the glory of God. And not only that, but we also boast in our sufferings, knowing that suffering produces endurance, and endurance produces character, and character produces hope, and hope does not disappoint us, because God's love has been poured into our hearts through the Holy Spirit that has been given to us" (Romans 5:1-5).

"Justified," "faith," "peace," "God," "Jesus Christ," "access," "grace," "hope," "sharing," "glory"—these are great words. But what is "we also boast in our sufferings" all about? People who talk like this can jar you to the fillings of your teeth like an eggshell left in the potato salad. A cheery "Smile, Jesus loves you" at a really bad moment can make you stand up, yell "Go away!" and slam the door. Solomon observed, "Like vinegar on a wound is one who sings songs to a heavy heart" (Proverbs 25:20).

Paul, however, is not saying that suffering is a great thing, for there is no grace or glory in hurting deeply or having your heart broken. He is speaking rather to a specific knowledge that arises from the experience of suffering that can be obtained in no other way.

This point was succinctly stated by my 5-year-old, Andrew, the day he helped me by hammering a nail into a board. The hammer hit his little thumb. He looked up at me in dismay at this new and unpleasurable experience. "How are you doing?" I asked anxiously.

"I'm OK," he said. "But I don't want to do this anymore."

What is suffering? It is pain, brokenness, loss experienced over a period of time. We ask about a deceased loved one, "Did she suffer?" Oftentimes the pain does not lead to the mercy of death. We live out our days and hours with torn hearts and anguished minds. But as the sun rises and sets repeatedly, the thought slowly seeps into our soul that we are surviving. That is the product of suffering identified by Paul—endurance. Hurting plus living is the algorithm of endurance. We do not know how it happens, but we keep waking up and another night has passed with its loneliness and terror, and there we are—enduring.

This endurance, said Paul, will produce character. *The New American Standard Bible* uses the phrase "proven character." What is character? The keys that I strike to compose this message and the letters in the words on this page are characters. A character is a symbol. A character stands for something. The kind of character produced by endurance of suffering is inherent in the process of a life of adversity. Earl Palmer finds an illustration of this character development in the growth cycle of a certain tree.

"At the timberline of Mount Shasta, California, lives a remarkable tree called the Shasta Fir *(Abbies magnifica, shastinis)*. In its early life it is twisted and almost brushlike. The heavy snowpack, which often amounts at timberline to more than twenty feet during the winter months, batters and presses the young plants so that they twist and turn and struggle to survive. There comes a winter, however, when this tree is able to establish itself through the snowpack—and begins to point skyward like an arrow. Once this victory is won against and through the snow, its vertical straightness is then unmatched by any other alpine tree. The tree is all the more impressive in the summer when you see the twisted and oddly shaped parts of the lower trunk. The snowpack has done its best to distort and crowd and harass, but when the time is right, the Shasta Fir wins out over the crushing weight of snow and gale force winds. The vertical is all the more impressive in the face of the odds against it" *(The Enormous Exception* [Waco, Tex.: Word, 1986], p. 56).

It is at the point when a life breaks free from what would oppress, distort, and destroy it and points skyward straight as an arrow that the character of that life is produced and proven. Paul said that character produces hope. Hope! This is a bit unbelievable, isn't it? We traverse the sorrow, the pain, the fire, the flood, and even shed blood, and then stagger out into the dawn with hope? What hope could possibly arise out of such misfortune?

Lewis Smedes helps us understand this hope with the following wonderful story:

"One early evening as the dusk darkened the always shadowed Sistine Chapel, Michelangelo, weary, sore, and doubtful, climbed down the ladder from his scaffolding where he had been lying on his back since dawn painting the chapel ceiling. After he had eaten a lonely supper, he wrote a sonnet to his aching body. The last line of his sonnet astonished me when I first came upon it at an exhibition of the master's sketches and the memory of it has comforted me in my times of self-doubt: 'I am no painter.'

"But when the sun shone again, Michelangelo got up from his bed, climbed back up on his scaffold, and labored another day on his magnificent vision of the Creator at work on His brand-new world. What pushed him up the ladder? Could it have been anything but a hope born again from a night's rest, a hope just strong enough to keep the doubts in check for another day, a hope that became the energy to paint the greatest picture of them all?" (*Standing on the Promises* [Nashville: Thomas Nelson], pp. 28, 29).

Smedes defines hope this way: "Hope is a gift waiting for all who have a powerful wish for life to be better than it is, the imagination to look beyond the bad that is to the good that can be, the faith to believe that the good they imagine and wish for is possible" (*ibid.,* p. x).

Ragtag, thirsty wanderers that we are, what stops this hope from being nothing but an illusory mirage that things are going to be better? As a business attorney I spend much time extricating hustlers and the hustled from the false hope of material security through quick riches. The hardest thing about this is that people want to believe in alchemy, in some magic formula that only the wealthy and elite possess, the Midas touch that will create heaven on earth. The poorest among us purchase the most lottery tickets.

Well, Paul said, the process that takes us through suffering to endurance to character to hope will not leave us with a hope that disappoints us "because God's love has been poured into our hearts through the Holy Spirit that has been given to us." Often mysterious in its truth and power, never magic, but always real, God's love is the secret to the endurance of suffering. The love of the Creator, who cares enough to return as Redeemer, is what is symbolized by the character that results from the endurance. The love of Christ—who became poor that we might be rich in love, who left a throne in heaven to pitch His tent in our neighborhood and experienced our most human sorrows and gained a firsthand acquaintance with our griefs, whose healing hands were pinned to splintered wood by spikes, who hung suspended on a Roman cross until the downward pull of gravity and weight of broken humanity combined to literally burst His heart—the love of Christ, who was broken and given for us, is poured into our hearts so that they may keep beating in the assurance that we are loved now and forever in spite of it all.

Now, there is a remarkable thing about God's love applied to our broken hearts. When we eat bread or a muffin, we break it open to increase the surface for the spread we place on it for flavor and nourishment. A broken biscuit can receive more butter and jam. To break a heart is to increase its surface capacity for love. When Christ broke bread with the weary, sad disciples at Emmaus, their hearts "burned" within them with His love and new hope (Luke 24:30-32). When Christ broke morning bread on the beach for His disciples, whose dreams had been demolished by His crucifixion and who were listlessly fishing to pass the time, they took heart and regained their purpose and capacity for love (John 21).

The surfaces of Jesus' heart broken in love for us meeting the surfaces of our hearts broken with love lost to us. This is the starting point of hope. It is right here at ground zero of grace that all who receive Him as their hope, who believe in His name, receive Christ's gift of power to become children of God (John 1:12). Friend, if you're wondering *Can this be true?* here is a sure word of grace for you from a man who sinned greatly and found greater grace, who loved and lost and found a deeper love: "The Lord is near to the brokenhearted, and saves the crushed in spirit" (Psalm 34:18).

TWENTY-EIGHT

The Grace of the Second Chance

*A teenage boy and a corporate lawyer receive
the blessings of forgiveness and affirmation.*

Jesus told this story about the grace of the second chance:

A man had an apple tree planted in his front yard. He came expecting to find apples, but there weren't any. He said to his gardener, "What's going on here? For three years now I've come to this tree expecting apples and not one apple have I found. Chop it down! Why waste good ground with it any longer."

The gardener said, "Let's give it another year. I'll dig around it and fertilize, and maybe it will produce next year. If it doesn't, then chop it down" (see Luke 13:6-9).

In my junior year of high school I participated in a dishonest prank that threatened one of the hallowed traditions of the private church academy where I was enrolled. Eight hours of intense faculty meetings followed during the next three days as the faculty debated my discipline. Some thought I was worthy of redemption and argued to give me a second chance. Others felt I was a bad influence, insubordinate, and a sneak who deserved to be made an example to the student body. I was ashamed and afraid. Those who wanted the harshest punishment prevailed.

I was standing in the hall of the administration building when the last meeting ended. A young English teacher, Mr. Walls, came out the door first. He strode down the hall to me, put his arm around my neck, and pulled my head tight against his shoulder. After whispering a rather feisty word of encouragement, he walked quickly out the door to his 1969 Chevy Camaro. When he drove away he burned rubber down a half block of driveway.

The next year he sought me out before the school year started. He was the adviser to the student newspaper. "I want you to be the editor," he said.

"Me?" I asked, amazed.

"Yes, you. Pick a staff and let's get started." That's all he said, but it was enough. When some of the faculty criticized his choice, Mr. Walls and the new principal stood their ground and sheltered me. It gave me a fresh start and led to a happy, successful senior year. It taught me a lesson in the grace of the second chance.

Years later I was a young attorney with a big corporate client. Some of the most important employees and officers of my client proposed a scheme whereby they would manage an important asset of the corporation without disclosure of the profits to the board. I wrote an opinion letter disapproving the transaction in strong terms, warning the board that it had a fiduciary obligation to keep informed and oversee the corporate assets. The powerful leader of the group making the proposal stood before the board and ridiculed me. "I don't know why I need to defend myself to our own attorney. He just doesn't get it," he said at the end of his remarks. The board voted, and my position was rejected.

Emboldened, the same group sought my ouster as corporate counsel. "He's too cocky." "He really doesn't understand what we need to do." These were some of the milder criticisms. The president of the corporation took a lot of heat, but he supported my retention. Then he announced his retirement, and I lost my protector. The new president had a chance to pick his own counsel and was expected to do so. The corporation was an important client of my law firm. The loss of its business would be a career-limiting event for me.

The new president called and invited me to lunch. It was a week before he took office. "This is it," I thought.

He came by himself and picked me up at my office. He took me to lunch at a nice restaurant. We talked about his plans for the future and baseball, which we both love. At the end of the meal he leaned over the table and looked me in the eye. "I know what they are saying about you," he said, "but I want you to know that you are my attorney." He shook my hand to seal the deal and never mentioned it again. The group of critics soon left the corporation. My professional career is anchored in that moment of the second chance.

More years passed. I was part of a legal team for the same corporation that advised a high-risk strategy in defense of a lawsuit. Although the case was not lost, the strategy failed under withering criticism from an appellate court that complained of overzealous advocacy. It is my responsibility to give a legal affairs report to the corporate board at each meeting. I decided to tell the board members what had happened, without excuse. They always hear the news of successes from me and depend on my word for guidance. I could not stint on the bad news and expect to maintain credibility. I told them what happened.

"We are officers of the court," I said. "We take your representation as an honorable organization seriously. Speaking for myself and my colleagues, we are chagrined to have brought this criticism upon you. You have our apology. Are there any questions?"

The room was silent. I looked out at the board members, many of whom were old friends and mentors, who were used to my glowing reports of transactions successfully concluded and courtroom triumphs. *What will they think? What will they do?*

I took my seat in the quiet. The chairperson went to the next item on the agenda. A surprising thing happened. A board member stood on the other side of the room. A director for many years, he is a wealthy business executive known for his blunt speech and tough questioning. He walked around his colleagues and across the spacious boardroom. He came to where I was seated and stopped. There he stood beside me for the rest of the meeting until adjournment. He walked out of the room with me. He never said a word. He didn't have to speak. The grace of the second chance needs no words.

King David reached midlife in wealth and power. In his self-indulged malaise he lusted for Bathsheba, who was married to one of his loyal soldiers, Uriah. When the resulting pregnancy could not be covered up, David had Uriah murdered and married Bathsheba. Guilt consumed David, and he tried to cleanse his conscience by becoming more religious. Church attendance and lavish offerings could not ease his guilt or stop the talk about what had happened. He was confronted with his sin and the consequences by the prophet Nathan. "You deserve to die. The child of this affair will die. Your household is going to be dysfunctional and troubled" (see 2 Samuel 12).

David confessed his sin in anguish. He admitted that his religious efforts were just a whitewash of his misdeeds and a pretentious attempt to gain God's favor. "For you have no delight in sacrifice; if I were to give a burnt offering, you would not be pleased. The sacrifice acceptable to God is a broken spirit; a broken and contrite heart, O God, you will not despise" (Psalm 51:16, 17).

Somehow God's forgiveness soaked into this hard, ravaged mess. David had many wives. He could have written off Bathsheba as a bad idea, as a reminder of how low he had sunk into depravity. But mercy truly received is mercy to be given. This is the grace of the second chance. David stayed with Bathsheba. He comforted her in the loss of their son. He had ruined her life and reputation by his insistence on the affair and his murderous scheme. Now, in the grace of God's mercy to him, he loved Bathsheba and consoled her. She conceived another child, and, although David named him Solomon, the God of the second chance sent another name, Jedidiah—"Beloved of the Lord" (see 2 Samuel 12:24, 25). In the genealogy of Jesus are found David and Bathsheba (as the wife of Uriah; Matthew 1:6). Jesus Christ is the ultimate second chance.

I don't know about you, but I am the tree in Jesus' story. I failed expectations and blew first chances. The grace of the second chance has been extended to me more than once. Receiving it can be devastating. It means I'm not in control. I need a second chance, and someone else has to give it to me. It requires me to just stand there while someone prunes me back. Sometimes I have to stand in some pretty stinky stuff to enable new life and growth. I am grateful for every one of my second chances, and most of all for the risen Lord of the second chance.

Jesus Christ *is* our second chance. I have heard Brennan Manning say, "God expects more failure from us than we do from ourselves." He writes:

"What makes authentic disciples is not visions, ecstasies, biblical mastery of chapter and verse, or spectacular success in the ministry, but a capacity for faithfulness. Buffeted by the fickle winds of failure, battered by their own unruly emotions, and bruised by rejection and ridicule, authentic disciples may have stumbled and frequently fallen, endured lapses and relapses, gotten handcuffed to the fleshpots and wandered into a far country. Yet, they kept coming back to Jesus" (*The Ragamuffin Gospel* [Portland, Oreg.: Multnomah, 2000], p. 176).

Child of grace, do you need a second chance? Is the ground that you started on, that you thought was so stable under you, now dug up and turned over? Are you standing in "stinky" stuff? Consider the possibility that the Gardener of your life, who knows your faults and inadequacy and loves you as you are and not as you should be, is telling you, "Here is an opportunity for growth. Let's see what a chance for the roots to breathe and some manure spread around will do." I will testify to you of my personal knowledge that if you can accept the truth of this proposition, you have a second chance in Jesus Christ and you are on your way to fulfillment of that chance in eternal love and life.

TWENTY-NINE

Beauty Is Never Wasted

From the bottom of the wastebasket and a broken alabaster box
come the truth that no extravagant response to grace is ever wasted.

Patricia bought a small wastebasket for our study. It has an elliptical shape squared off on one end. I noticed something unusual in the canister when I removed the plastic wrapper. It was a piece of cardboard cut to the shape of the wastebasket and fitted in the bottom. Written on it in Old English type were these words: "To what purpose is this waste? Matthew 26:8."

This surprised me. I looked up the text in my Bible and read this story:

"While Jesus was in Bethany in the home of a man known as Simon the Leper, a woman came to him with an alabaster jar of very expensive perfume, which she poured on his head as he was reclining at the table.

"When the disciples saw this, they were indignant. 'Why this waste?' they asked. 'This perfume could have been sold at a high price and the money given to the poor.'

"Aware of this, Jesus said to them, 'Why are you bothering this woman? She has done a beautiful thing to me. The poor you will always have with you, but you will not always have me. When she poured this perfume on my body, she did it to prepare me for burial. I tell you the truth, wherever this gospel is preached throughout the world, what she has done will also be told, in memory of her" (Matthew 26:6-13, NIV).

Who left the King James version of this text in the wastebasket? Clearly it was authorized by the manufacturer. Was the message intended to be a plea for recycling? Did it represent an opportunity taken to proclaim the gospel in homes and offices by stirring curiosity? Was it a biblically literate joke by the manufacturer?

There are different accounts of this anointing in the Gospels (Matthew 26:6-13; Mark 14:3-9; John 12:2-11). Luke records a distinctly different account of a woman washing Jesus' feet with her tears, drying them with her hair, and dressing them with ointment (Luke 7:36-50). Some scholars say all accounts refer to the same event. Others say that Luke refers to a woman thanking Jesus for forgiveness, and the other accounts refer to a separate act of worship. Whichever the case, Jesus' reaction is one of great tenderness and appreciation. He thought enough of the action to say its description would always accompany the telling of the gospel throughout the world.

The disciples were miffed, because they didn't deem the act useful. It was a waste of money, they thought. John placed the value of the perfume at a laborer's wages for a year. He blamed Judas for the comment, saying that Judas wanted money in the disciples' treasury so he could steal it (John 12:5, 6). It was an extravagant, lavish act, and it offended the utilitarian sensibilities of the accountant, commercial fishermen, and political activists that made up Jesus' retinue.

Is an act of devotion ever a waste? Martha thought Mary was wasting time when she was talking to Jesus instead of helping out in the kitchen (Luke 10:38-42). There is always some project calling for our time and attention, some cause to claim our energy and ability. I have discovered over the years that Martha has many more defenders than Mary. Someone has to fix lunch, even if no one asked for lunch. Our driven selves cry out to anyone who will listen—if you can't measure it, time it, quantify it, package it, label it, clean it, make it, evaluate it, or store it, what good is it? Stirring in the debates that swirl around worship styles is the thought that singing praises to God or spending time alone with Christ in solitary prayer and contemplation is a luxury and an indulgence that detracts from the real work of the gospel. Never mind that Jesus went off to pray whenever He could, that the decisive moments of Scripture occurred during, or were preceded by, encounters with God in solitude by Abraham, Jacob, Moses, Joshua, Samuel, Elijah, David, Isaiah, John, Peter, Paul, etc., or that Judah was triumphant when its army entered battle behind a choir singing hosannas to the Almighty. That was nice for them. They were writing the Bible, but now someone has to execute the plan.

My family loves music. My dad has a beautiful tenor voice. My mom plays a creditable piano. We all learned the piano and another instrument, and our home life kind of played out as a musical. My parents emphasized to us that music should glorify God and it did that when it was played with competence (practiced skill) and honest feeling (touch). When I was 13, I played the French horn in our church orchestra. There was a trombone player named Ken who was a superlative musician. He was college-age and was working in a local hospital to earn enough money to complete his education. He was a mature Christian who had suffered much in reaching adulthood. One night after orchestra practice he started to practice for a solo that he was going to play for the church service. It was a breathtakingly elegant classical piece. Midway through, the pastor stopped him. I listened in shock as the pastor told Ken that he couldn't play the piece during the worship service. "Why?" Ken asked.

"Because that song doesn't have words," said the pastor. "No instrumental solo should be played in church unless the congregation knows the words of the song." The experience of beauty in the composition and the performance as an offering to God was totally lost on the pastor. He didn't exactly say "For what purpose is this waste?" but he clearly meant it. To him, and many others I've encountered since then, if it isn't practical, it has no place in the church. The very glory of grace, however, is that it isn't practical. You can't plan grace, budget grace, earn grace, or balance grace. You can only show up, receive it, and say thank you.

In Ken Follett's *Pillars of the Earth* there is a moment described that moves me. A medieval cathedral is burned down by arson while it is under construction. A master builder and architect named Tom approaches Prior Philip with bold plans for a new cathedral with a radical, soaring design. Here is Follett's narrative of the conclusion to Tom's heartfelt presentation of his drawings. Prior Philip asked Tom:

"'You want to build this cathedral yourself, don't you?'

"Tom hesitated. It was well to be candid with Philip: the man had no patience for prevarication. 'Yes, Father. I want you to appoint me master builder,' he said as calmly as he could.

"'Why?'

"Tom had not expected that question. There were so many reasons. *Because I've seen it done badly, and I know I could do it well,* he thought. *Because there is nothing more satisfying, to a master craftsman, than to exercise his skill, except, perhaps to make love to a beautiful woman. Because something like this gives meaning to a man's life.* Which answer did Philip want? The prior would probably like him to say something pious. Recklessly, he decided to tell the real truth. 'Because it will be beautiful,' he said.

"Philip looked at him strangely. Tom could not tell if he was angry or something else. 'Because it will be beautiful,' Philip repeated. Tom began to feel that was a silly reason, and decided to say something more, but he could not decide what. Then he realized that Philip was not skeptical at all—he was moved. Tom's words had touched his heart. Finally Philip nodded, as if agreeing after some reflection. 'Yes. And what could be better than to make something beautiful for God?' he said" (New York: Signet, 1990, pp. 293, 294).

The anointing of Jesus was excessive, surprising, and fragrant. It was a gift, and the woman had to give it. It was grace. Estimating the cost of a gift or criticizing the giver for not putting the money to better use is never a gracious act. Put it in the context of the popular MasterCard commercials. "Feeding the poor, always an opportunity. Fragrant oil of pure nard, 300 denarii. Alabaster box, 25 denarii. Preparing Jesus in love for burial, priceless."

I spend hours a week writing e-mail messages about grace. Why? I ask myself. It leaves me vulnerable. It may presume upon my friends' goodwill and invade their cyberspace. There is always a nagging question—is this just ego? Am I writing to pontificate? Are these words a waste of perfectly good silence?

On one of our evening walks I asked Patricia why she thinks I write these messages. She answered, "Because of the same reason I break into songs of praise in the middle of the day when no one is around. My heart is full, and I have to praise. Your heart is full, and you have to write." She's telling the truth. I have to write about the grace of the God I know. The old hymn goes: "Sing the wondrous love of Jesus, sing His mercy and His grace." When I write to you I am singing His song, maybe not always on key, maybe not always with comprehensible lyrics or useful formulas, but I'm singing as David sang: "Worship the Lord in the beauty of holiness" (Psalm 29:2).

I am grateful to the devoted manufacturer who pointed me to Christ from the bottom of a wastebasket. Beauty is never wasted.

THIRTY

Queen Kandice

A little girl discovers the love of God in a small group Bible reading.

I caught a fresh glimpse of grace one Friday evening in the living room of my friend Joyce. It flashed in the smile of an 11-year-old foster child named Kandice during a small group fellowship and Bible study.

We've met in that living room every other Friday night for more than 10 years. There are nine of us in the group, including four original members. Others have come and gone, but not one meeting has been missed.

The group started in 1991 as a response to a sermon I gave on the need for real love and mutual support in our congregation. Our church was encouraging groups to form at that time as part of a growth plan. It even obtained a grant for training group leadership. I went through the leadership training and read six books on group dynamics. The trainers and the books said a group like ours doesn't last beyond two years. Well, after two years of praise and worship, searching study of the Word, prayer for one another, and real encouragement in our walk with Christ, we were still going. So I threw out the books, and we thrived.

The key ingredient to our group's success is a hunger for God. It can't be manufactured. If a person has it in their soul, you can read it in their eyes and in their determination to know Christ better. There is no second best to them. Sit down in a living room with people like that, and Christ will be the natural subject of conversation. Grace flows in that setting.

Sue has belonged to the Friday night group for eight years. She recently retired as an engineer for a major aerospace company. Her life has been marked by harshness and adversity. The night that she discovered God's love she was warmed and joyful as she had never been. She stayed awake all that night and the next, fearing that the wonderful presence would leave her.

Sue has lived mostly alone since childhood. She's suffered from

Crohn's disease, an inflammatory disease of the intestines that increasingly ravages her body with pain and blood loss. It can be contained but not cured, and it is fatal if unchecked.

Over the years Sue became sicker and very frail. Then one Friday night in November 1997 she made a quiet prayer request at the end of the meeting. She was up to an astonishing 66 milligrams of steroids a day to control the inflammation. She was in extreme and constant pain. Her liver was sustaining damage from the medication. Her doctor said there wasn't any more to be done. She announced that she was going to die.

The Holy Spirit spoke to my heart: "Anoint her; lay hands on her and pray for her healing." I found out later that two others, Joyce and Rosie, had had the same thought. There was urgency to doing it right then, but I thought, *Sue loves her church, and her pastor and head elder should be involved,* so we waited. On Monday I contacted the head elder, and the following week after the church service our group members showed up in the pastor's study for a healing service.

We walked in from three denominations and four congregations. The pastor was really surprised that we existed at all. The church leadership had changed over the years and lost interest in small groups. The church had long since forgotten that we were out there. Where once there had been 15 home fellowship groups, three remained. We've stayed Christ-centered and positive, making no challenges to congregational authority or affiliation. Our two steadfast rules are respect for each other's confidences and no discussion of church politics (a sure way to death for a small group). "The squeaky wheel gets the grease," and we didn't squeak. No committee or pastor had come looking for us.

We spoke our favorite verses over Sue. The pastor anointed her forehead with olive oil. We laid hands on her and prayed in the name of Jesus in the earnest, comfortable way of believers who have been praying and taking Communion together for years. Engineer to the core, Sue went home and diagrammed where everyone had been standing so that she would remember this special moment of love.

December saw no improvement in her condition, but she was alive, and I realized that God was doing this. He is Sue's healing. He is her life.

She came to a group meeting in January from an appointment with her physician. Her blood tested clear. The inflammation was gone. The physician asked what happened. Sue told him, "Prayer. Jesus did this." The physician didn't believe her. But something happened. Today she is clear of manifestations of the disease, but her bemused physician still has her on a daily dose of 2 milligrams of anti-inflammatory medication.

One Friday night I drove up to Joyce's house. Surprised to hear the sound of children, I called Joyce out. "What's going on? Are there kids inside?"

"We've a few," she said.

"Who are they? I see Sue. Are they hers?"

Before Sue retired she had applied to adopt two foster children. She had been accepted, but none of us had yet met the children.

Inside I met Kandice, a dark-haired, dark-eyed 11-year-old with dimpled, skinned knees and a dazzling smile, and Valentine, a blond, blue-eyed 5-year-old girl. When I introduced myself, Kandice was reserved in response, which told me it was likely that she had known few adult men, and those whom she did know were suspect. The 9-year-old grandson of another member was also present.

We settled down, and I started with prayer and opened the discussion of Jeremiah 7. Valentine had clearly never been in a setting like this, and kept fidgeting and moving about. It was kind of distracting.

I kept trying to move the discussion along, breathing a prayer of thanks that at least we were studying the life of an 8-year-old king, which might have some appeal to the children. Josiah rediscovered a copy of the "lost" book of Deuteronomy when he authorized a cleanup of the Temple in Jerusalem. This led to a revival that Jeremiah knew didn't go far enough into the hearts and lives of the people. Jeremiah's insights about true revival were the focus of our evening's discussion.

Kandice had a Bible, and I noticed that she looked up the texts as we discussed them. The rest of the time she looked from one face to another as if unsure what this was all about.

Sue was clearly on edge with the newness of motherhood in her 50s and the restlessness of Valentine.

I asked the question "If you were seeking to introduce an 8-year-old like Josiah to God, would you read to him from the book of Deuteronomy? It's the book of the law. It can be pretty tough going in parts."

I pointed out that we can't disdain the effect of such a reading. It is the

Holy Spirit that illuminates and inspires the Word in us. And we are to nurture seekers after Christ from whatever point that ignites their interest. To buttress the point, I thought of the experience of Philip with the Ethiopian eunuch who was struggling to understand the prophecies of Isaiah. Philip took him right from that point and guided him to Christ. This story supports the proposition that we help people from where we find them, and we may miss out if we first try to turn their attention to other scriptures that are more to our liking. I impulsively said, "Please turn to Acts; I'm not sure exactly where yet."

As I flipped the pages, I saw Kandice diligently looking for the text. I tried to get Sue's attention by gesturing to ask if Kandice could read the text, since she was next in the circle. Sue didn't look up.

So I asked, "Kandice, would you like to read?"

She nodded soberly.

"Please read Acts 8, verses 26 to 40."

She began to read in a clear, strong voice these words: "Then an angel of the Lord said to Philip, 'Get up and go toward the south to the road that goes down from Jerusalem to Gaza.' . . . So he got up and went. Now there was an Ethiopian eunuch, a court official of the Candace, queen of the Ethiopians, in charge of her entire treasury."

When she read the name "Candace" she paused and gasped, "That's my name." My heart somersaulted in my chest.

Joyce said, "Whoa. How about that!"

Kandice flashed a wide smile. We all smiled back at her. Her eyes widened in wondrous delight. She realized in that instant that God knows her name. "It is going to be OK," her whole expression said. "I really belong." She was home!

I had forgotten that the queen's name was Candace. But God hadn't. It doesn't matter that the spelling is different. It sounds the same. It means a lot, especially to an 11-year-old girl two weeks into foster care in her new home, with a new mom, in a group of adults talking about strange things. Jesus Christ blazed before our eyes in Kandice's smile of recognition. He didn't forget her, and He didn't forget us in sharing the joy of His claiming the little girl as His own. Remember that God said long ago: "Can a woman forget her nursing child, or show no compassion for the child of her womb? Even these may forget, yet I will not forget you. See,

I have inscribed you on the palms of my hands" (Isaiah 49:15, 16).

Just another night of grace in the family of God. It always keeps me coming back for more.

THIRTY-ONE

We Mourn Because We Love

A grieving heart reveals a legacy of love.

There is perhaps no greater challenge to faith than the death of a loved one. It is easy to ask, on such an occasion, Martin Luther's question: *"Where may I find the gracious God?"*

Several years ago a close friend asked me to give the homily at the memorial service for his brother, a young physician who was also a friend of mine. This is not a common request to an attorney, and it compelled me to sit down and struggle with what I really believe about God, death, and eternal life. I share some of those remarks with you here in the hope that you will be encouraged and strengthened by them.

When everything is said and done, there is nothing stronger than love. It endures all things and it bears all things. Love always hopes. Love always trusts. Love lasts! (1 Corinthians 13:4-7).

Those waves of pain and grief that sweep across you when you least expect it are your loved one calling you in loving memory. Jesus said, "Blessed are they that mourn: for they shall be comforted" (Matthew 5:4). He thereby told us that if we can feel the deep things, weep the real tears, and truly grieve the loss of our beloved, God's heart of love will enfold us and fulfill the promise of love.

Jesus confronted the death of His dear friend Lazarus by weeping, and He weeps with us in our loss (John 11:33-35). King David, no stranger to a tumultuous life of loss and brokenness, contemplated the heart of God and wrote, "Precious in the sight of the Lord is the death of his saints" (Psalm 116:15). Your beloved is precious to our Lord, and so are you. Christ's gentle hand of mercy extends to you to hold you in this moment when all seems to be falling apart and lost.

Listen carefully to God's Word:

"Who will separate us from the love of Christ? Will hardship, or distress, or persecution, or famine, or nakedness, or danger, or sword? . . . No, in all these things we are more than conquerors through him who loved us. For I am convinced that neither death, nor life, nor angels, nor rulers, nor things present, nor things to come, nor powers, nor height, nor depth, nor anything else in all creation, will be able to separate us from the love of God in Christ Jesus our Lord" (Romans 8:35-39).

Is it true?

Death brings questions. Can we honestly speak of the death of our loved one and the love of God in the same breath? How can we who loved this person, some from birth, some from childhood, go on from this moment to work, eat, sleep, and do the thousand other things that mark our days?

The essential truth of Christianity is this: Humans were made to be loved and sustained by their Creator. Our original ancestors tried life on their own apart from the Creator. Being created beings, they lacked the power to sustain their own life. The result was separation from God and death. God the Son, our Creator, came to earth and lived and died as a human in full identification with our flesh, our blood, our common colds, and our heartaches. He laid Himself down as the bridge of reconciliation between our finite, futile existence and the eternal. He died because most people who knew Him could not believe that God wanted to forgive rather than seek vengeance, and they would rather eliminate this disconcerting possibility than believe it. The power of the Father raised the Son from death, and because He represented us, as the prototypical human, the power of death was destroyed for all who accept His life as their life. It is all for love, because God loved us so much that He removed all barriers between us so that we could reconcile and live together forever. So eternal life—the life that transcends the tears and grief here and now, the life that lives beyond the grave, the life that will bring our broken bodies up from the grave when Jesus returns to take all those who trust Him home to heaven—that life is not a matter of what we do or don't do. Eternal life is found in knowing, accepting, and reconciling with the one who has defeated death for all of us.

But are these just words? If this is true, why does our heart ache so? Because ultimately, there are no answers; only a love that will not let us go. In the words of Henri Nouwen:

"The resurrection does not solve our problems about dying and death.

It is not the happy ending to our life's struggle, nor is it the big surprise that God has kept in store for us. No, the resurrection is the expression of God's faithfulness to Jesus and to all God's children. Through the resurrection, God has said to Jesus, 'You are indeed my beloved Son, and my love is everlasting,' and to us God has said, 'You indeed are my beloved children, and my love is everlasting.' The resurrection is God's way of revealing to us that nothing that belongs to God will ever go to waste. What belongs to God will never get lost—not even our mortal bodies. The resurrection doesn't answer any of our curious questions about life after death. . . . But it does reveal to us that, indeed, love is stronger than death. After that revelation, we must remain silent, leave the whys, wheres, hows, and whens behind, and simply trust" (*Our Greatest Gift: A Meditation on Dying and Caring* [Harper Collins, 1994], pp. 108, 109).

Love is stronger than death! We prove that when we gather to remember our departed loved one because even though he is gone, the memory of love is enough to bring us together.

The great Chinese preacher Watchman Nee wrote:

"Why mourn? Because there is love. Without love there can be no mourning, for there will be no such reaction where love is absent. Without love, there will be neither crying nor mourning. This then is a test" (*Interpreting Matthew* [Christian Fellowship Publishers, 1989], p. 70).

Love is more than equal to the test of death. Solomon at the conclusion of his Song of Songs wrote to his lover: "Set me as a seal upon your heart, as a seal upon your arm; for love is strong as death, passion fierce as the grave. Its flashes are flashes of fire, a raging flame. Many waters cannot quench love, neither can floods drown it. If one offered for love all the wealth of his house, it would be utterly scorned" (Song of Solomon 8:6, 7).

So what our loved one leaves us is love. Our loved one's life was lived in many roles: child, sibling, lover, spouse, parent, and friend. But the sum of all of these is love. We receive his legacy in the memories and stories of that love.

In my vocation as an attorney I have stood beside many bedsides in intensive-care units and sat around hospital conference tables while family members made the agonizing decision of whether or not to terminate the artificial life support that was keeping the lungs breathing and heart beating of a terminally ill loved one. I have been in that position myself. The overwhelming observation that I take from those moments and share with you now is this: Tell the people that God has placed in your life that you love them. Tell them now while they are living, and tell them often.

Let there be no doubt that you love them and forgive them for any hurt they have caused you and seek their forgiveness for any pain that you have caused them. Those who leave these doubts, who allow resentments to smolder and eat away hearts in this life, are those for whom no consolation will suffice, no words will comfort, and who in their despair and desperation can cause so much distress and distraction for others who are grieving. Even if this is the case for you, do not lose hope. God who holds the future and the power of forgiveness is always listening to hear your prayers and to extend grace and cleansing to the stained and brokenhearted.

John, the beloved disciple of Jesus, wrote: "No one has ever seen God: but if we love one another, God lives in us and his love is made complete in us" (1 John 4:12, NIV). God is released into our lives through forgiveness and reconciliation. Forgiveness and reconciliation free all of us to the possibility of talking with our loved one in the eternal tomorrow. It is never too late for God. "'I am the Alpha and the Omega,' says the Lord God, 'who is, and who was, and who is to come, the Almighty'" (Revelation 1:8, NIV).

God lives for each one of us with an unconditional power that transcends our sorrow and gives us hope beyond this death. Those of us who reach out to the Jesus Christ that our loved one knew and embraced, learned at mother's knee and in dad's prayer; the Jesus who blessed our loved one with reconciliation and hope in the midst of the painful life search for love and significance—those of us who know *that* Jesus know the assurance of being together with our loved one forever.

The apostle Paul once wrote to a group of discouraged Christians in Thessalonika, Greece. They had accepted Christ in the hope that He would come soon to take them from this world. When He hadn't come, some were tortured for their belief, some died, and some drifted away from faith into their former worldly way of life. "What's happening?" they asked Paul. "How will this end?" Paul's letter in reply contained these words:

"We do not want you to be uninformed, brothers and sisters, about those who have died, so that you may not grieve as others do who have no hope. For since we believe that Jesus died and rose again, even so, through

Jesus, God will bring with him those who have died. For this we declare to you by the word of the Lord, that we who are alive, who are left until the coming of the Lord, will by no means precede those who have died. For the Lord himself, with a cry of command, with the archangel's call and with the sound of God's trumpet, will descend from heaven, and the dead in Christ will rise first. Then we who are alive, who are left, will be caught up in the clouds together with them to meet the Lord in the air; and so we will be with the Lord forever" (1 Thessalonians 4:13-18).

Forever! We will be together with the Lord forever, and that is enough!

Nothing—not death, not the demons of doubt and insecurity, not numbing grief, not the darkness and pain of sorrow—can separate us from the love of God in Christ Jesus. The Holy Spirit of God calls out to you to believe this. "Anything is possible if a person believes," Jesus said to a distraught father one day (Mark 9:23, NLT). All things are possible if a person believes! In this moment when you justifiably may feel unable to choose or give anything, simply receive the gracious love of your loved one's Savior and yours.

Believe that Jesus Christ has taken care of all of the past—whatever losses, mistakes, and sins are there. Believe that Jesus will take you through this hour and the days ahead until you reach the promised place where time shall be no more and we will dwell with our loved ones in the presence of our heavenly Father forever. Do you want this? Do you want this with all of your heart? Then simply tell God that is what you want and receive it. It is God's gift to you! It is God's love for you! It is stronger than death.

Jesus lives! You will see your loved one again.

THIRTY-TWO

Who Pays the Check at the Father's Table?

*A loving father demonstrates his love
for his children in a true parable of grace.*

My son,' the Father said, 'you are always with me, and everything I have is yours'" (Luke 15:31, NIV).

My dad, Ted Hansen, will celebrate his ninety-second birthday February 22. He built things: auditoriums, dams, bridges, dairy barns, dormitories, but mostly houses—cozy, comfortable, strong homes for families, with lots of windows. Dad loves the outdoors and thinks the best houses are on a hill and have plenty of windows.

Dad's lap was the safest, warmest place I've ever known. He would come home smelling like salt sweat and sawdust. After pulling me up in his arms and hugging me, he'd tell me stories and laugh. He would frequently lead us in the Lord's Prayer at the end of our nightly family worship. When we said, "Our Father," it was his smile and deep-set blue eyes I would think about. What a wonderful difference this view of God has made in my whole life and the lives of my brothers and sister.

Years later our mom suffered an illness that brought all four of us home—Teddy, the eldest; Judi; Terry; and me, the youngest. We met Dad and went with him to Mom's bedside to encourage her before surgery.

Miles and years had separated us. The experiences of life had altered our courses and changed our appearances. But love for our parents drew us together into that hospital room with smiles and hugs.

Later, when Mom was in surgery, we all went to lunch with Dad at the local café. We were easy in each other's company, joking with the server while we ordered, exchanging stories as we ate sandwiches and omelets.

The server brought the check and handed it to Dad. Immediately our hands went to our wallets—radiation technologist, interior designer, hospital administrator, and attorney—each ready to prove our goodwill and worth by paying the tab. "Let me get that, Dad." "I'll take care of this!" "You don't have to pay, Father." "Please, give it to me." Our voices overlaid one another's with demands to help.

Dad shook his head no as his gnarled, work-scarred fingers pulled bills from his worn wallet. Those fingers and that wallet had sacrificed to ensure our church school and college educations, giving us the success that we were now so eager to demonstrate. He did not have to do more for us.

But he wanted to do more. "Listen to me," he said in the firm, kind voice that had guided and comforted each of us through a thousand troubles. "I'm your father. You're in my territory now. I pay the bills for you."

Our eager expressions of capability and pride were hushed by the simple, eternal truth that a loving father always cares for his children, no matter what they have become or where they have been. The memory of this fact is what brought the prodigal to his senses to say, "I will set out and go back to my father" (Luke 15:18, NIV). The alternative, as Paul pointed out, is bleak: "Or do you show contempt for the riches of his kindness, tolerance and patience, not realizing that God's kindness leads you toward repentance?" (Romans 2:4, NIV).

In the territory of grace, our Father always provides the meal and picks up the check. Stop fighting Him for it. His heart's desire is to pay the bill. Let Him do it for you and just say "Thanks."

THIRTY-THREE

Grace for the Crazy Woman

Sometimes we lose our mind in devastation of loss.
The only antidote is grace.

She was labeled from the start, named for Magdala, a hometown of no account except her notoriety. She was a woman of strong, conflicting passions. Her demons drove her. She stood out in a society that liked its women to be quiet in public. An unmarried woman seeking a life of her own pays a high price. Unable to characterize her in any other way, they called her a "whore," although the record is devoid of any evidence supporting this conclusion.

"Who am I?" was a question that haunted her. No one, including her, knew who she really was. You could see her at least seven different ways: "She's crazy"; "She's possessed"; "She's angry"; "She's evil"; "She's a tramp"; "She's mean"; "She cares about no one but herself"; "Just look at her. Who does she think she is, anyway?"

We don't know how she encountered Jesus. One day she showed up, demons gone, peaceful and healed in the company of women following Jesus. It was a very personal story, a moment too sacred for words. But she knew this was life and love as she had never known. Even as her heartache eased, her determination to follow surged, and others took note.

These were days of delight. The lame leaped and ran, the blind saw, the deaf heard, the mute spoke, and the sick glowed with restored health. There was too much to be absorbed. Jesus loved her and treated her with respect. There were no jokes or put-downs on her womanhood. He answered her questions with intelligent conversation. The second miracle for her was the acceptance from women who wouldn't have given her the time of day before they met Jesus. Now society women such as Joanna, wife of the king's steward, and Susanna, and many others rich and poor, young and old, took her in and graced her with their companionship. It was safe there.

Then they killed Jesus. They came and got Him as He prayed at night. By the next morning He was on the way to execution. "They" were the men in charge, the priests, the scribes, the rich Pharisees. In the crowd, yelling, "Crucify Him, crucify Him," were some who had called her "whore." *They are so afraid of difference and love,* she thought. *Grace-killers.* And the joy seeped from her heart and ebbed from her soul.

What can you do when the life you have always wanted and finally have is ripped to shreds in front of you? When hands that gestured to you with tenderness are crushed, and when the arms extended to you in welcome are stretched out in cruel parody? When the one who cooled your fevered desires with understanding cries out in desperate thirst as the life drains out? And when you go back to look for that life all you find is an empty, gaping black hole. You feel lost, that's what.

In that moment of lostness, when all that is good and light and warmth personified have left you searching when you never thought you would have to search again, the question rises, as it did for her, "Is it the gift or the Giver that matters?" This question came to Abraham at the altar, and to Jacob while night wrestling. It comes to my friend who struggles with doubt even as her husband strays. It breaks in roller-coaster waves over the young mother who watches her infant intubated and monitored in the neonatal intensive-care unit, struggling to find traction on the new path of life. And it came to Mary before the empty tomb. The question of judgment, the question of grace demands to be asked—"Is it the gift or the Giver?" You ponder the question, looking at the gaping black hole in your life, in your soul, in anguish, thinking *It wasn't supposed to be this way. Where is my Lord? Where is my God?*

Then it is that the unexpected Jesus asks ever so softly, "Why are you weeping? Whom are you looking for?" (John 20:14).

From a place in your heart so deep that, but for this very moment, you would never know that it is there, the answer wells up, *"I want the Giver* and nothing less"—and you demand, "Tell me where He is, and I will carry Him away with me."

"Mary," Jesus calls out to her. Once He had told her and the others, "It isn't that I can make you invincible and impervious to hurt—Oh no! What counts is that I know your name" (Luke 10:17-20, paraphrase). Everything you thought you knew for sure crumbles in your mind when the God of the universe personally speaks your name. From that point on and forever, what you will know and believe and receive is embodied in the one you now call "Teacher" (John 20:16).

The instruction of eternal life begins when you realize Christ knows your name and you yield to Him as teacher. "Don't hold on to Me," is His surprising first word. "Don't hoard My truth in miserly pockets of fear. Go and tell your brothers and sisters that I go to My Father, who is your Father, and My God, who is your God. We are in this together, and there is enough of Me to go around" (John 20:17, paraphrase).

I have known Jesus Christ from my childhood. I have been a sold-out follower of Him for the past 13 years. Like Mary, I know Christ is present in the power of the Holy Spirit when I leave a gathering in His name with a bigger picture of God than I brought with me and my love for God and for my brothers and sisters has increased. Any teaching or experience that diminishes and depersonalizes God, reduces our love, or emphasizes the gift over the Giver is not of the Spirit and is to be shunned.

Child of grace, whatever they may have called you, Jesus knows your name. The fading bloom of first experience may disillusion you. The life and love you have longed and struggled for may be lost to your sight in the darkness of misunderstanding and contempt. Let go of the gift. Take the Giver, and there will be grace enough for your greatest need and more to pass on. If the Giver is not enough for you, ask yourself, "Why not?" The answer to that question yielded to God will be a sacrifice pleasing and acceptable to Him.

Mary left that place to tell the others that Jesus had risen. In that moment, at the start of a new day of a new world, this woman of no account but great devotion was the entire confessing church. All things are possible to the one who believes.

THIRTY-FOUR

Launching Into the Dark

A revelation of the gospel received on a trip across the water

The first song I ever learned and my favorite as a child was about Jesus sailing across Galilee. Its chorus went like this:

> Rock, rock, rock,
> Little boat on the sparkling sea,
> Rock, rock, rock,
> Dear Jesus rides in thee.
> Rock, rock, rock,
> O'er the waters swiftly flee,
> For Jesus rides in the little boat
> On blue Galilee.

> —Barbara Knox-Albertswirth, 1915

The disciples Peter, Andrew, James, and John fished on Galilee. They loved to spend the night on the water. The Gospels record that night was their preferred time for fishing. Jesus would accompany them sometimes and found peace and rest while the boat was underway in darkness (Mark 4:38). Despite some tough experiences with storms, they returned to the sea at night again and again even after Jesus was crucified (John 21:3).

Most people come to the sea during daylight for the view. It is night when the sea can be experienced as a living thing. Fish run and feed then. The foam can glow with phosphorescent organisms. The darkness reveals the tiniest light, and the absence of sight magnifies the sound of the wind and waves. Current and air respire fog. This is the world experienced at its most elemental.

I grew up on the Pacific Coast and learned to love the water at night. It is a place to think without distraction. One night in college I rowed a life raft out into the middle of a Sierra lake in the moonlight and slept there.

I was invited to give the devotional talks for a pastors' retreat on Catalina Island in late January one year. The retreat site was a camp accessible only from the sea. We left Avalon Harbor by launch on a Sunday evening and ran along the east coast of the island. There were 30 or so of us in the boat, talking and laughing. It was clear, and the sea was calm. In the distance we were coming up on lights, brighter than a football stadium. They were squid boats that use banks of lights to attract their catch. The surface of the sea and the coastal cliffs looked like the day.

There was something else in the dark sky overhead. Hundreds of stars were sparkling and swirling. What were they? The effect was stunning. Our conversation quieted. With careful watching the outlines of wings could be seen behind the lights. The swirling stars were the eyes of wheeling seagulls reflecting the lights from the squid boats.

There are singular moments of grace in nature. I have heard others describe theirs—a glittering ice cave in Iceland; the smell of the coming monsoon rain in the highlands of Sonora, Mexico; a star-lit night sky so perfectly reflected in the still waters of a Texas lake that it was impossible to tell where the sky left off and the water began. This was such a moment. We looked at it with hearts prepared for three days of prayer and fellowship, and we were welcomed into the presence of God.

One of the pastors beside me, a veteran of great heart and humble spirit, said to himself as much as anyone, "I'll never again wonder why the disciples loved the water at night."

Our boat rounded a point back into the darkness, but each of us knew the delight of being in the presence of one who knows each of His creatures down to the common sparrow and notes their falls with compassion. "He heals the heartbroken and bandages their wounds. He counts the stars and assigns each a name. Our Lord is great, with limitless strength; we'll never comprehend what he knows and does" (Psalm 147:4, 5, Message).

At night, in the darkness, at sea, far away from home, a heart aches for more. At night, in the darkness, at sea, without distractions, the heart can find its cure. I believe this is why Peter went fishing after Jesus died. He went out on the dark water in grief and found reconciliation with his resurrected Lord on the beach in the morning. At the end of his life he wrote of the need to be attentive to the hope of Christ "as to a lamp shining in a dark place, until the day dawns and the morning star rises in your hearts" (2 Peter 1:19).

There are indeed singular moments of grace and breathtaking encounters with Jesus. We might never know them if all we do is come to the shore by day for the view. We might never know them if we never launch out into the dark with our God who creates, counts, and names the stars for delight and heals our heartaches and bandages our wounds for love.

THIRTY-FIVE

Curses, Sighs, Groans, and Other Prayers

*A woman tells God that she hates Him
and discovers His love for her in return.*

There is a myth that God hears only prayers that use the "right" words. What I mean by the right words are nice, reverent, positive words and phrases. The idea that prayer requires such words is hogwash dished up by pious perfectionists who want to sell how-to books and keep you scared enough to listen to their "all stick and no carrot" theology.

My friend Joyce had had enough! Years of surviving abuse, abandonment, illness, marital betrayal and divorce, bills, kids in trouble, and bad religion had taken their toll on her self-esteem and a once-vibrant relationship with God. She went home from work and climbed in the shower. There she screamed out to God, "I hate You! I hate You!" She poured out the anger and bitterness of her heart in curses as the hot water washed over her.

She stepped out and toweled off. In the silence a question rose in her soul: "You aren't dead, are You?" It surprised her. All her life she had thought that if you talked that way to God, He would strike you down.

The next day her landlord was working in her backyard. He came to the back door and called to her, "Come see what's out here." She stepped out across the lawn, which had been mowed just a few days before. There, rising up out of the grass, was an unusual flower. It had a long stem supporting six deep-pink and white trumpet-shaped blossoms with bright yellow stamens. It was perfect. It hadn't been there two days before when the lawn was mowed. How had it grown so fast? How did it force itself through the root thatch of the lawn? Why was there only one? So many questions, and great beauty. She knelt beside it and gently cupped the blossoms in the hollow of her hand. She was delighted. In that moment God spoke to her heart, "See, that's what I think about you. You are unique. You are beautiful in My sight. I delight in you." Life and spirit flooded back into her heart and mind as she stood up in the restoration of the Lord.

My friend's experience is authentic grace. Even now, long after this happened, if someone in our small group, where she first told this story, mentions "Joyce's flower," it brings instant smiles and tears of joy.

Crying out in pain that you hate God has this to commend it—it is honest. God can handle honesty. It also confronts the One who has the power to do something about the pain. We project our anger and spill our angst all over people, but all this shows is that misery loves company. When our children skin their knees they insist on telling us about it. No one but Mommy or Daddy will do at such a time. No one can listen, hug, and place the band-aid like a parent. So our kids bite their lip and grit it out until they can dissolve their tears and upset in our arms. We are children of a heavenly Father. It works the same way with Him. This is the premise of many of the psalms.

There are people of my acquaintance who hate to read the psalms. They say that they are too full of hurt, struggle, betrayal, anger, and disappointments. "Bloodthirsty," one person described them to me. The psalms are gritty because they are real prayers prayed by real people in the highs and lows of their life.

A few years back I was called by a friend, a longtime executive who had been devastatingly and treacherously betrayed, threatening his good reputation and career. He was upset beyond words. I suggested that he read Psalm 109 before he went to bed that night. This is a prayer of David that reads:

> Do not be silent, O God of my praise.
> For wicked and deceitful mouths are opened against me,
>   speaking against me with lying tongues. . . .
> In return for my love they accuse me,
>   even while I make prayer for them.
> So they reward me evil for good,
>   and hatred for my love.
> They say, Appoint a wicked man against him;

let an accuser stand on his right.
When he is tried, let him be found guilty;
    let his prayer be counted as sin (Psalm 109: 1-7).

May his days be few;
    may another take his place of leadership.
May his children be fatherless
    and his wife a widow
May his children be wandering beggars;
    may they be driven from their ruined homes.
May a creditor seize all he has;
    may strangers plunder the fruits of his labor.
May no one extend kindness to him
    or take pity on his fatherless children.
May his descendants be cut off,
    their names blotted out from the next generation.

May the iniquity of his fathers be remembered before
    the Lord;
    May the sin of his mother never be blotted out. . . .
May this be the Lord's payment to my accusers,
    to those who speak evil of me.
But you, O sovereign Lord,
    deal well with me for your name's sake;
    out of the goodness of your love, deliver me.
For I am poor and needy,
    and my heart is wounded within me (verses 6-22, NIV).

My friend told me the next day that this prayer helped save his spiritual life by allowing him to bring his feelings of hurt and betrayal to God. You may ask why a prayer like this is even in the Bible. It's there for two reasons. It shows us that we can pray about anything, even when we are angry, and there are texts that say we can even pray our anger and disappointment with God. (See Psalm 77:6-9; 102:6-11; 44:13-16; 88:1-18.) David did the best thing that he could do with his anger—he put the problem squarely in God's hands.

It doesn't matter that the words weren't nice. Jesus taught that greeting-card formulas for prayer are worthless. He said, "When you are praying, do not heap up empty phrases as the Gentiles do; for they think that they will be heard because of their many words. Do not be like them, for your Father knows what you need before you ask him" (Matthew 6:7, 8).

The apostle Paul told the Romans this principle of prayer: "The Spirit helps us in our weakness. We do not know what we ought to pray for, but the Spirit himself intercedes for us with groans that words cannot express. And he who searches our hearts knows the mind of the Spirit, because the Spirit intercedes for the saints in accordance with God's will" (Romans 8:26, 27, NIV). God is so ready, willing, and able to hear and answer our prayers that He accepts the groans and sighs of an honest but desperate heart as prayer, and He has a plan for exactly the help that we need. A great writer on prayer said, "Pray as you can, don't pray as you can't" (Dom Chapman, in Brennan Manning, *The Ragamuffin Gospel*, p. 155).

Sometimes it is impossible to pray in words at all. When my sister was diagnosed with pancreatic cancer, almost immediately her body reacted with increased thrombin in her blood. This created a clot that exploded like a grenade in her brain. It deprived her of speech and the use of the left side of her body, and in three awful weeks she was dead. But at first she could recognize and respond to her loved ones.

On the third evening after the stroke I slipped into her hospital room and sat beside her holding her hand. When the lights were turned down for the night, I began to softly sing to her the hymns and songs of our life. She gripped my hand firmly in her right hand and somehow she moved her limp left arm over her body and laid that hand on top of mine. I sang "Precious Lord, Take My Hand," "My Faith Looks Up to Thee," "Turn Your Eyes Upon Jesus," "Shall We Gather at the River," "In the Sweet By and By," "In a Little While We're Going Home," "It Is Well With My Soul," "God Leads Us Along," "My Jesus, I Love Thee," "What a Friend We Have in Jesus," "Sweet Hour of Prayer," "Jesus, Keep Me Near the Cross," "Holy, Holy, Holy," "I Must Tell Jesus," "Near to the Heart of God," "Hear Our Prayer, O Lord," "Jesus Loves Me," "Gleams of the Golden Morning," "Day Is Dying in the West," and more. In between songs I would pray aloud for our heavenly Father to hold and comfort her and touch her with His love. I thanked Him for the many joys that we had shared. With my free hand I stroked her dear forehead. From time to time I would think she was asleep and would start to gently pull my hand away. But her eyes would open and she would grip my hand more tightly. We were siblings from a family that loved to worship. This was the sacred threshold of eternity, where life and death come together in their sunset. The songs and the touch were prayer. The hushed peace of our loving Savior enveloped us in the darkness. His presence was the answer to her speechless, waiting heart.

These words of Ole Hallesby have great meaning to me:

"We will all have use for wordless prayer, if not before, when the death-struggle and the death-agony tax all our energies. That does not always take place exactly at the moment of death. The death-struggle is usually fought out some time before the end comes.

"I have witnessed the death-struggle of some of my Christian friends. Pain has coursed through their bodies and souls. But this was not their worst experience. I have seen them gaze at me anxiously and ask, 'What will become of me when I am no longer able to think a sustained thought—nor pray to God?'

"When I stand at the bedside of friends who are struggling with death, it is blessed to be able to say to them, 'Do not worry about the prayers that you cannot pray. You yourself are a prayer to God at this moment. All that is within you cries out to Him. And He hears all the pleas that your suffering soul and body are making to Him with groanings which cannot be uttered. But if you should have an occasional restful moment, thank God that you have already been reconciled to Him, and that you are now resting in the everlasting arms'" (*Prayer* [Minneapolis: Augsburg Press, 1994], p. 150).

The apostle Paul observed that there are times when we don't know what, or how, to pray. In these moments, he said, the Holy Spirit intercedes for us "with sighs too deep for words," and God translates those sighs of longing into prayer (Romans 8:26, 27). God hears the honest, not the merely articulate.

THIRTY-SIX

Heart of Love Enfolding All

*The incongruous juxtaposition of a Benedictine monastery and a
marine base provides insights into God's gift of peace.*

David prayed:
> Where can I escape from your spirit,
> where flee from your presence?
> If I climb up to heaven, you are there;
> if I make my bed in Sheol, you are there.
> If I travel to the limits of the east,
> or dwell at the bounds of the western sea,
> even there your hand will be guiding me,
> your right hand holding me fast.
> If I say, "Surely darkness will steal over me,
> and the day around me turn to night,"
> darkness is not too dark for you
> and night is as light as day;
> to you both dark and light are one (Psalm 139:7-12, REB).

Dwelling at the bounds of the Pacific Coast of North America, as I
have my entire life, has made vivid to me these words of David about the
encompassing presence of God.

Never have they meant more than on an August evening. I sat in silence
in the church of the Prince of Peace Abbey, a Benedictine monastery located
on a bluff above the Pacific in Oceanside, California. I was waiting for com-
pline, the quiet time of prayer and liturgy that ends the monastic day.

It was 6:50 p.m. when I entered the silent church. I was seeking a time
of reflection and worship during a late-summer break from the external
pressures of deadlines, decisions, and conflict that fill my days as an attorney and the internal tensions a Christ follower experiences dealing with a
world that is not my home.

The orange sun rolled down the gray ramparts of the evening fog gathering at sea. The nearly full moon ascended over the Laguna Mountains as if a counterweight connected by rope and pulley to the descending sun. I thought of how Psalm 89:37 describes the moon: "The faithful witness in the sky" (NIV).

In the stillness I read a passage from Matthew and prayed to my Abba about its meaning for my life. Then I sat and pondered the final moment of the setting sun, distorted by angle and water into a fiery figure-eight and then a mushroom.

The end of the day and the coming of the night were revealed by the sweeping glass wings of the church. The windows were open to the mild dusk. The prevailing northwest wind blew off the water and carried the fragrance of coastal sage and eucalyptus through the sanctuary.

But my soul was still restless within me. Perhaps, I thought, it was the discordant hum of helicopter gunships beginning their night maneuvers at Camp Pendleton, the largest Marine base in the world, located next door. Maybe it was that I thought the service began at 7:30 p.m. and became impatient when that time passed with nothing happening.

In growing inner turmoil, my mind began to travel back to knotty problems of work, still-raw irritations of the past weeks, mistakes made, sins committed, slights received, and offenses given. Muscles tensed, adrenaline seeped, as my focus left the reverence of the present to wander away to past problems and future speculation.

I fought against the tide of anxiety and resentment with prayer. "Jesus," "Savior," "Redeemer," "Lord of my life, take control." "Father in heaven, may Your name alone be holy in all the earth and may I be conformed to Your holiness. Your kingdom come, Your will be done. . . ." It was a battle. "Why am I waiting around here?" I muttered. "I could be doing things."

Yet I waited, and at 7:40 p.m. a robed monk pushed a wheelbarrow full of sunflowers into the church. He rolled its balloon tire up the side aisle and to the altar. There he knelt and changed the flower arrangement. He pushed on around to various points, pausing to bow and pray from time to time, then he returned to tending to the arrangements with new blossoms or a sprinkle from a water can.

Watching this incongruous scene unfold focused me. It was a blessing to watch this devout young man quietly go about his service, faithfully attending to a menial task to the glory of God. A cricket began to chirp rhythmically in the corner. It was a welcome sound of praise.

Out the window, the evening star appeared above the approaching fog bank. The moon continued to rise. Lights were coming on along the coastline below the church.

As this all settled into my observation, a song that I have sung thousands of times since childhood surged up and through my heart, breaking over and drowning my remaining anxious thoughts:

> Day is dying in the west;
> Heaven is touching earth with rest;
> Wait and worship while the night
> Sets her evening lamps a–light
> Through all the sky.
>
> While the deepening shadows fall,
> Heart of love, enfolding all,
> Thro' the glory and the grace
> Of the stars that veil Thy face,
> Our hearts ascend.
>
> Holy, holy, holy,
> Lord God of hosts!
> Heaven and earth are full of Thee;
> Heaven and earth are praising Thee,
> O Lord most high!
>
> —Mary A. Lathbury, 1877

This hymn of soaring praise to a loving, trustworthy God has been sung by my family at Sabbath sunset for nearly 70 years. We have sung it on the beaches of Pacific islands, and on the Atlantic coast, where the sun sets over land. We have sung it at the crest of the Sierras and the Swiss Alps, in a basement in Maryland, on the plains of Kansas, around our piano, and in the family car far from home. Sometimes we've been so drained by loss and torn by pain that we've sobbed the words. Most times it is sung in joy and family solidarity in the worship of the Creator and Redeemer of our lives, whose ways we acknowledge as best even before the gathering and palpable darkness of the night and the uncertain prospect of the next dawn.

Now, in a monastery church, on a hill above the Pacific, watching a monk go about his duties as the lights of heaven and earth came on in the night, the song echoed with new meaning within me. *So this is what it means to "wait and worship,"* I thought. Even amid the sounds of helicopters and artillery in the distance perfecting the violence that is the best solution humanity can devise, Christians faithfully come together in the hopeful anticipation that God will deal with the world and the night. As we wait for the eternal dawn, we quietly work and praise and worship God. This night Psalm 4 was sung to end the day:

> Answer me when I call,
> God, the upholder of my right!
> When I was hard pressed you set me free;
> be gracious to me and hear my prayer.
> Men of rank, how long will you dishonour my glorious one,
> setting your heart on empty idols and resorting to false gods?
> Know that the Lord has singled out for himself his loyal servant;
> The Lord hears when I call to Him.
> Let awe restrain you from sin;
> while you rest, meditate in silence:
> offer your due of sacrifice,
> and put your trust in the Lord.
> There are many who say, "If only we might see good times!
> Let the light of your face shine on us, Lord."
> But you have put into my heart a greater happiness
> than others had from grain and wine in plenty.
> Now in peace I shall lie down and sleep;
> for it is you alone, Lord, who let me live in safety (REB).

The gentle, antiphonal voices of the monks concluded with a benediction of glory to the triune God and hope for the return of Christ and life in the eternal "world without end." They filed out to their cloistered rest.

155

I walked out into the moonlit silence that cannot be improved upon as a prayer. I realized again that as I dwell at the boundary of the western sea, the Lord most high of the universe, who touches both heaven and earth with the hand that creates and the hand that saves, sees through the darkness to account for the sparrows in their nests and the hairs of my head. Secure in that heart knowledge, I slipped redeemed and free into the darkness, and I prayed with David:

> Lord, you have examined me and you know me.
> You know me at rest and in action;
> you discern my thoughts from afar.
> You trace my journeying and my resting-places,
> and are familiar with all the paths I take.
> For there is not a word that I speak
> but you, Lord, know all about it.
> You keep close guard behind and before me
> and place your hand upon me.
> Knowledge so wonderful is beyond my grasp;
> it is so lofty I cannot reach it (Psalm 139:1-6, REB).

THIRTY-SEVEN

Giants

A little boy finds God an ever-present help in facing his terror of bicycles and reveals the deep truth of grace.

At its heart most theology, like most fiction, is essentially autobiography. Aquinas, Calvin, Barth, Tillich, working out their systems in their own ways and in their own language, are all telling us the stories of their lives, and if you press them far enough, even at their most cerebral and forbidding, you find an experience of flesh and blood, a human face smiling or frowning or weeping or covering its eyes before something that happened once. What happened once may be no more than a child falling sick, a thunderstorm, a dream, and yet it made for the face and inside the face a difference which no theology can ever entirely convey or entirely conceal" (Frederick Buechner, *The Alphabet of Grace* [San Francisco: Harper San Francisco, 1989], pp. 3, 4).

"One of the strange things about the language of religion and theology is that it does not permit itself to be used. The reason for this is fairly clear. It is not something neutral, a mere instrumentality. When we use such language simply for the sake of using it, the result is sheer nonsense, garbled communication. The language of religion is the vehicle of collective experience and it is meaningful only when it speaks of experience and addresses itself to experience" (Dorothee Soelle, *Death by Bread Alone* [Philadelphia: Fortress Press, 1978], p. 31).

We gave our son, Andrew, a bicycle for his sixth Christmas. He went with me to pick it out. It was orange and green and perhaps too big for him. I put training wheels on it, and he practiced throughout the winter and spring. With summer, the training wheels came off and Andrew began to fall.

The bike brought out Andrew's incipient perfectionism. He wants to do things right the first time or not at all. After a couple of spills, he didn't want to ride anymore.

Patricia and I made Andrew ride. Retreating to the alley behind our home, Patricia pushed Andrew to start. I stood 20 yards away to catch him. He rarely made it. He would panic and look at everything but the road in front of him. When the bike wobbled, he would stop pedaling and tumble into the neighbor's rose bushes, fences, garbage cans, power poles, and whatever else lined the alley. We dried his tears, but we made him get back on and try again.

"Everyone learns to ride a bike," I told him. "Once you learn, you will never forget."

"I don't want to learn," he snapped.

"Yes, you do. It's fun."

"No, it's not!"

So it went week after week. One Sunday afternoon the crashes were so hard and the arguments so tense that I started to put the training wheels back on.

"Don't," Patricia said. "He needs to learn to ride on two wheels, and once he starts we don't go back." I agreed. It is a tough truth, but surrender to gravity is never a good option in bike riding or in life.

The next week at church, Andrew went to his class. When we picked him up afterward Patricia asked him, "What did you learn today?"

"The teacher told us about David and Goliath."

"What did she say?"

"Goliath was a giant. He teased the Israelites and made them feel bad, but God helped David kill him with his slingshot."

Then Andrew held out a piece of paper. "The teacher gave us this picture of Goliath. She asked us to draw the 'giant' in our life that scares us most so we can ask God to help us get rid of it."

Patricia and I stopped on the sidewalk and looked at his picture. There on Goliath's breastplate was a crude but clearly drawn bike, and beside it was a little boy in a bike helmet, wide-eyed, with teeth clenched in terror.

The picture broke our hearts. We hugged Andrew and went home. The bike-riding giant was the subject of many parent/child prayers and eventually was slain. The picture was placed in a desk drawer as a memento of a true battle of faith.

Two years later I sat in a restaurant with my friend Richard. He is an attorney who eats lunch with me every Friday so that we can discuss spiritual matters of interest to us. On this particular Friday he brought along Bill, another attorney acquaintance.

As we began our conversation Bill announced, "I think all of the Old Testament is prophecy."

"Really," I said. "I suppose I agree in the sense that the Old Testament points to Christ. But on what specific evidence do you base this belief?"

"Well, take the story of David and Goliath. I believe that it is prophecy of how the apostate church will be overcome by the faithful remnant in the last days."

"Where do you find that interpretation in the Bible?" I asked.

Bill's reply was sharp. "Well, there's nothing that says it isn't true."

"Think about it," I said. "You're a lawyer. Your training tells you that you can't prove a negative proposition. You can't show what is by what is not."

Bill shifted ground. "All these things are open to interpretation. The teacher of the Bible class my wife and I attend says that David's rock symbolizes the gospel, and Goliath's forehead represents human reason that will be struck by the gospel just before sinners die in the judgment."

Richard asked Bill, "Where does your teacher get that idea?"

There was an edge to Bill's voice. "It kind of makes sense, doesn't it?"

I was distressed. These lunches were usually blessed times of insight and encouragement. I did not enjoy this argument.

"Bill," I asked quietly, "don't you think the story of David and Goliath stands for the basic truth that in God's power we can overcome the enemies that oppress us?"

"Well, yeah, I guess so."

I knew it was so, because in my desk drawer was a picture of a terrified little boy beside a bike—a picture drawn in vulnerable hope and simple faith that God would help him overcome the giant that he faced. Andrew's exegesis convinced me.

Jesus said, "I praise you, Father, Lord of heaven and earth, because you have hidden these things from the wise and learned and revealed them to little children. Yes, Father, for this was your good pleasure" (Matthew 11:25, 26, NIV).

Lord, thank You for the unadorned truth of Your good news revealed in our experience.

THIRTY-EIGHT

The Grace of Goodbye

Sometimes the greatest blessing is the ability to say goodbye.

My sister, Judi, was diagnosed with serious breast cancer. She asked me to stand with her through the surgery and treatments that followed. The next weekend I attended a group prayer session and requested prayer for my sister. I sat in a chair while the others laid their hands on me and prayed for her. Peace entered my heart in the Holy Spirit's assurance that God was commanding the situation and that my sister would not die from the tumor. I told Judi, and she was comforted. The cancer was surgically removed, and she returned to health.

Years passed, and Judi was diagnosed with pancreatic cancer. The physicians said it was unrelated to the breast cancer. Judi and I talked daily for the next week as she began to rally herself for the fight ahead. Then, before the final diagnosis was received, Judi suffered a cancer-related stroke. I sat beside her hospital bed at night, held her hand, prayed over her, and sang to her. In those night hours in the hospital and then at home in hospice care, peace again blessed my heart, but this time it was the peace of a "goodbye." An earthly life that was full and well-lived was ending.

Why was my heart encouraged with the knowledge of her healing the first time, but at rest with the knowledge of her impending death the second time? Do I have a special hot line to God? Did I lack faith the second time?

These are good questions to which I have no answer, except that God is loving and kind and dispenses peace as a sign of His will. "Let the peace of Christ rule in your hearts" (Colossians 3:15, NIV) wrote the apostle Paul. The Greek word that he used for "rule" means the call of an umpire or referee. Sometimes that call is that the game is over. I have slowly learned to seek Christ's peace and yield to it.

This isn't just a question of health. It arises in our work and our relationships as well. We can battle on in pride and stubbornness and fear. Or

160

we can say our goodbyes, moving ahead day by day, trusting God to lead us to the only place that counts—the place that He has prepared for us. John 14 finds Jesus saying goodbye to His disciples and them resisting the change that His leaving will mean. "Where are You going?" "How can we know the way?" "Show us the Father." "How will You reveal Yourself to us when You return?" are some of their desperate and concrete questions. "I will prepare a place for you," He tells them. "I will come again." "I am coming again." In John 16 Jesus tells them, "It is good for you that I am going away, because then the Holy Spirit can bring to your minds and hearts the full perspective on who I am and who you are with me."

Solomon wrote: "Better is the end of a thing than its beginning; the patient in spirit are better than the proud in spirit" (Ecclesiastes 7:8). There is great grace in an honest goodbye. I have watched many men and women decide whether or not to turn off the artificial life support of loved ones, and many more leave their jobs or self-destructive relationships. The key, I've observed, to weathering the passage is forgiveness. Those family members who have stated their love in honest and direct terms and who have not kept the tether of unforgiveness tied to the past are able to allow their loved ones to pass away in peace. Those employees who do not insist on self-justification and the vindication of their pride can move on in the provision and assurance of a gracious God who does not forsake the righteous or reduce their children to begging for bread (Psalm 37:25). Those men and women who do not think another warm body will make them whole, who give up the effort to try to undo the pain and shame of the past by burying themselves in a new relationship, can receive with open hands the freedom and worth implicit in the love of God and they can move on in the lives that He recreates in mercy.

Goodbyes are doorways to mercy, compassion, healing, and grace. Without goodbyes "there are no reunions, no fathers running down the road toward children who have been away, no neighbors crowding around to celebrate the finding of a lamb that has just come home on the shoulders of the shepherd." The man who introduced me to this last thought wrote those words several months after release from a mental hospital where he had been admitted for suicidal depression. His name is Robert Benson, and he wrote one of the most original books on the Christian experience that I've read. Even the title is wonderful: *Between the Dreaming and the Coming True: The Road Home to God* (New York: Putnam Publishing Group, 2000). Listen to Benson's beautiful meditation on the grace of saying goodbye:

"I was in the hospital around Easter, and the doctors gave me a pass to go to church on Easter morning. My sister came to pick me up and help me get there. Sitting in the pew that morning, barely two blocks from the hospital where I was told I might well have been dead instead of alive on this Easter morning, it came to me that resurrection is a theological concept that may well be ignored unless one's death cannot be.

"It then follows that forgiveness is not much of a concept without something for which to forgive and be forgiven. Healing has no meaning in the absence of illness. Peace is no treasure at all to those who have known no war and no strife. Saying hello has no joy in it without the saying of goodbye.

"I am coming to believe that the thing God said just before 'Let there be light' was 'Goodbye, dark,' and that Noah could not say hello to the rainbow without first having said goodbye to the world as it disappeared beneath the waters of the flood. And that something deep and mysterious about saying goodbye from the bottom of a pit made the hello that Joseph spoke to his father all those years later all the more wondrous. 'Goodbye, Egypt' turned out to be another way for the Israelites to say, 'Hello, Canaan.'

" 'Goodbye, Jesus of Nazareth,' whispers Mary through her tears at the foot of the cross on Friday afternoon. 'Hello, Lord of the universe,' she murmurs to the one she mistakes for a gardener, on Sunday morning.

"Even Jesus Himself, the Word that was with God in the beginning, could not completely know the Father's love without leaving home. Until He came among us, God's goodbye ringing in His ears, Jesus could not know [the reality of receiving] providence or mercy or forgiveness or grace; He could not know the side of God that can be known only by those who have been away. He could not know what it was like to be missed, to be loved from afar, to be whispered to in the darkness of the wilderness or the garden or the tomb. He could not know what it means to recognize God's face in the sunrise or pray God's name into the glittering silence of the sky on a sweet summer night. He could not know what it means to see God in the face of a child or hear God in the rustle of the trees.

"Until there is goodbye, there is no hello. Until there is a journey away, there is no coming home" (pp. 37–40).

I write about these things in the holiday season when memories accelerate and we remember the goodbyes with which we struggled and never wanted to say at all. Just know this: Jesus said goodbye when He came for us and goodbye when He left us, and we know that He struggled with it. He knows our losses and longing. The last time He said goodbye, He also left word with two angels: "This same Jesus, who has been taken from you into heaven, will come back in the same way you have seen him go into heaven" (Acts 1:11, NIV). The last word of Jesus to His loved and His own will be hello. This is the gospel.

THIRTY-NINE

Don Kanen

A college student travels hundreds of miles and gives
selfless service to bring a classmate healing after a tragic accident.

The portrait of Christ drawn on the sheet of our life's experience is an outline something like those dot-to-dot books parents give their children to keep them quiet in church. What connects the dots is Christ's hand moving with a variety of instruments—prayer, worship, forgiveness, healing, friendship, suffering, and solitude. Sometimes we look back and glimpse what is taking shape and ask ourselves, "How did that line get filled in? I didn't even know what was happening."

God frequently uses His other children to sketch His face for us in artistry so subtle that each dot connected is not recognized as an essential element of the whole until long after it is drawn.

It is good to think about how the dots of our life have been connected in grace and about the creativity Christ has used to connect them. If we pray our thankfulness and wait with open hearts, our Abba may tell us a secret or two about who has helped to restore His image in us.

In this spirit, I share with you the story of a businessman from southern Colorado. Long before he was a business success, a husband, and a father, Christ selected him to draw a crucial line in the picture of my life. In all gratitude, I must acknowledge what this friend did as essential to the creation of the person who subsequently was so overwhelmed by the grace of God that I am compelled to proclaim His "relentless tenderness" to you.

Don Kanen was my classmate and fellow history major at La Sierra University (then Loma Linda University, La Sierra). While we were living in the same dormitory as sophomores, I became acquainted with Don as a hardworking, hard-playing guy with a ready laugh and an intense, direct approach to life. He was creative and a good photographer. When I was elected to be the editor of the student newspaper, *The Criterion,* for my junior year, I selected Don for the difficult task of layout editor.

Don and I liked each other and worked well together, but each of us had our own circle of closer friends. So we went our respective ways most of the time.

My childhood sweetheart and I became engaged two weeks into our junior year. We accepted a call to be student missionaries in Japan the next year. On October 19 we drove the 400 miles home to tell both sets of parents that we were engaged. On the way back home the next day I drove over a rise in the interstate, and on the other side was a stalled car. The collision killed my fiancé instantly and left me with torn legs and a broken heart.

The next few weeks were a blur of surgery, funeral, tears, condolences, and numbing despair. I went back to school out of an instinct for survival. However, doctors discovered that the damage to one knee was more severe than initially thought, requiring another major surgery for me to have any chance of normal use of my leg. I came out of surgery, wheelchair-bound, with a massive cast on my leg.

As my parents drove me home for the Thanksgiving holiday, none of us knew what the future held, or even how I could possibly complete the rest of the school year. La Sierra University has a beautiful hillside campus, but in 1973 it was not really wheelchair-accessible. There were many steps. All my classes were on the second and third floors of buildings. I roomed alone as a resident assistant for a dormitory floor. The cast would be on my leg for many weeks, and then there would be a difficult period of rehabilitation. I was in such shock that I could not think beyond each present moment.

The phone rang early on the morning of Thanksgiving. It was Don. He wasn't just checking in to see how I was doing. He asked if he could come to my house for the weekend. I asked my folks. They said yes. So I told him that he was welcome.

His coming to my home was no small feat for him. Not only was he giving up his Thanksgiving with his family, but he had to drive a long way to do it. I lived in Soquel, on California's central coast. He lived in Bishop, near the California-Nevada border. Between our homes was the Sierra Nevada range, which was impassable with snow in late November. Travelers in that part of the country wanting to go east to west must either make a long detour through the Mojave Desert to the south or around

Lake Tahoe on the interstates to the north. He drove his Datsun B-210 the southern route and arrived on Thanksgiving evening.

I was glad to see him. He got along well with my family, and we enjoyed visiting. The next day he loaded me up and took me for a ride. "I've come to get you to take you back to school," he told me.

"I don't know if I'm going back."

"Yes, you are."

"If I do go back, my parents will take me."

"I can take you. You need to be with your friends, and I'll get you there."

He talked to my mom and dad about it. They weren't sure, but Don was. He told them that he would look after me. They told Don that it was up to me.

I didn't know what to think. Here was this guy who didn't know me that well, appearing out of nowhere to pick me up and literally carry me back to school. And what then? I told Don my doubts. He had a gung-ho answer for every one of them. He told me that he had prayed about this, and this is what God had told him to do.

On Sunday we loaded up. He refused my dad's offer of gas money. My mom and dad prayed as my family and Don stood around my wheelchair. He helped me into the faithful Datsun, propped my leg up with pillows, and we were off.

It was a somber, overcast day. The radio news was devoted to Richard Nixon's announcement of gasoline rationing in response to the OPEC oil embargo. We drove down the San Joaquin Valley, over the Grapevine, around Los Angeles, and out to Riverside. There Don unloaded me into my room, helped me unpack, and took me out for our then favorite meal of Del Taco burritos. When he brought me back to my room, he answered my unspoken question. "I'll be here at 7:00 a.m. to help you dress and take you to class."

I couldn't figure out what we would do about my classes. The rooms were upstairs. My cast weighed nearly 60 pounds and was made to keep my leg folded, so that I was awkward to carry. Because my hip had been dislocated on the other leg, I was warned to use crutches as little as possible to keep pressure off. With these thoughts, I dozed fitfully through the night.

Don was at my door on time. He put my shoe on my one good foot, put my books on my lap, and off we went. He pushed me to a ground-floor classroom where I received another surprise. Each of my teachers had moved their class to the ground floor so my wheelchair could reach it. Don had arranged this. He also connected with other friends to take me places when he had to be in class.

Every afternoon Don came to my room and pushed me up the hill to another dormitory, where he worked as a resident assistant. His room had a suite with a bathtub—one of only a few in the whole school. He would help me undress and get into the tub so I could bathe and wash my hair. He did this for three weeks. This allowed me to keep up with my classes and continue editing the paper.

What Don really did was allow me to maintain my fragile grip on sanity. There was no such thing as normal for me anymore. I was a physical and emotional mess. Taking care of me took a lot of time that a busy college student did not have to give, but he gave it anyway. He never asked me for anything before or afterward. He never complained. The whole episode took place as if this was what was meant to be. This young man, without prequalification, condition, or reward, loved me. In those weeks Don did what no one else could do for me except the Christ who held him in grip—he gave me a bridge back to life.

The next quarter we eased back to our separate routines. I began physical therapy and went golfing with other friends even before I could stand without crutches. (One day we were "horsing around" and started to roll a golf cart over. I found out in a hurry that I could not only walk, but run again.) Don pursued other interests and friendships. After graduation he married Sue, another friend of mine from high school days. We lost touch with each other for a while.

Seventeen years later Don showed up at my law office. He needed help with the sale of one of his many business enterprises. I was glad to talk over old times and the in-between years and help him. He and Sue have a good life together raising a family in Colorado. Christ still leads them both to serve others in good cheer, and they follow. Don still takes on life with both hands.

In the darkness of November and December 1973, when I lost my future and my hope, unable even to walk, Christ came to me in Don Kanen. Christ also visited me in the La Sierra professors who disrupted their routines at great inconvenience so that I could keep attending classes. God bless them all! They are the reason parents are willing to pay more for Christian education.

When Jesus comes and tells Don what he did for Him, I imagine Don will ask, "When did I do that for You, Jesus?" (See Matthew 25:31-40.) I will be one of the answers.

Only Christ sees our dots that need to be connected. But once in a while He graciously lets us look back at the how and why and who. I look back, and one of the blessings I see is Don. I've thanked him before, and he's just brushed it off as no big deal.

But it is a "big deal." May we be encouraged to let Christ pick us up and use us to draw a vivid portrait of His love in the brokenness of another. This is my prayer.

FORTY

The Crossing

Jesus' baptism reveals the love the Father has for every one of us.

Then Jesus came from Galilee to John at the Jordan, to be baptized by him. John would have prevented him, saying, 'I need to be baptized by you, and do you come to me?' But Jesus answered him, 'Let it be so now, for it is proper for us in this way to fulfill all righteousness.' Then he consented. And when Jesus had been baptized, just as he came up from the water, suddenly the heavens were opened to him and he saw the Spirit of God descending like a dove and alighting on him. And a voice from heaven said, 'This is my Son, the Beloved, with whom I am well pleased'" (Matthew 3:13-17).

"When he entered the temple, the chief priests and the elders of the people came to him as he was teaching, and said, 'By what authority are you doing these things, and who gave you this authority?' Jesus said to them, 'I will also ask you one question: if you tell me the answer, then I will also tell you by what authority I do these things. Did the baptism of John come from heaven, or was it of human origin?' And they argued with one another, 'If we say, "From heaven," He will say to us, "Why then did you not believe him?" But if we say, "Of human origin," we are afraid of the crowd; for all regard John as a prophet.' So they answered Jesus, 'We do not know.' And he said to them, 'Neither will I tell you by what authority I am doing these things'" (Matthew 21:23-27, NIV).

Ripped through earth no older than any other, but ancient in the human history it supports, lies the gorge of the Jordan. There flows the river between the Sea of Galilee and the Dead Sea. Beyond the eastern bank, in those days, was the stark and rugged wild. To the west is the Promised Land, remnant of Eden, rich soil blessed by God through river, time, and toil.

It was there on the edge of the promise that John proclaimed the coming of the Messiah, sovereign of both those wild and those tamed. It was there at the water heart of life in the desert that John invited the stained and the thirsty to wash and to drink. It was the place of judgment between all that was of God and all that was not—between a land pregnant with promise and a land wasted and broken. It was a place of crossing. To such a place our souls are pulled by the gravity of eternity.

One morning Jesus came into this neighborhood. John's heart, anticipating this moment from before birth (Luke 1:41), rose up in his chest, lifting his eyes to the western bank where his cousin picked His way down the rocky path.

"Baptize Me," was Jesus' request.

"No, it's You who should baptize me," said John, dismayed by the Presence for whom his whole life was a preparation.

But this is the moment of crossing when the Son of God, who entered the world of humans as a diapered infant, now must enter the kingdom of God as all men and women must, by the door of necessary admission that no human initiative, capability, or power will open—the door that opens only by our assent that God and God alone is righteous.

This is one moment of history that my imagination bursts with longing to have witnessed. Did a hawk cry overhead in the warm updrafts above the cliffs? Did those watching hush as insects hummed the undertones of stillness? Did the cousins' bodies thrill to the cold of the water contrasted to the desert heat? Did they notice the hard stones beneath their wading feet, the mud squishing between their toes? Did John wonder at the mystery of touching God in the flesh, and did Jesus delight at the marvel of entering the life of creation as He had intended it to be before this world ever was (Ephesians 1:3, 4; Hebrews 1:1, 2)?

The crossing was made in seconds, the river's inexorable flow broken for the briefest of moments by a body slipped into it and out again. One question that must have stirred in both John and Jesus was "Now what?"

Heaven watched. The Father opened His hand and released the Holy Spirit as a dove, a creature both ubiquitous and defenseless, harbinger of peace to the young man so far from home. Then the Divine, unable to contain the love of an eternity, burst through the universe, tearing apart the blue fabric of the heavens, shouting in pride and joy: "This is My Son, whom I love and who pleases Me!"

To John, it was the fulfillment of the promise of his life. To Jesus, it was the affirmation that as a human, as a created being, He was loved and lovable to His heavenly Father, and He was therefore free to love. The knowledge seized His heart in a powerful twisting grasp that would release itself over time in loving compassion to the brothers and sisters who did not yet know that they were loved and lovable too.

This is the crossing of baptism as it was meant to be, from dark to light, death to life, from alienation to the full acceptance of God's love for the child rising from the water. The theologian Paul Tillich said the meaning of faith is "to accept the fact that I am accepted, in my total unacceptability." The baptism of Jesus by John represents a conversion, not from sin to righteousness (unthinkable for the Lamb of God without blemish), but in the radical refocus of Jesus' mind and soul through the revelation of the Father's love for Him. The receipt of this knowledge so altered Jesus of Nazareth with the wisdom of accepted tenderness that His townspeople who had known Him for years before His baptism questioned the obvious authority of graciousness that resulted.

"He came to his hometown and began to teach the people in their synagogue, so that they were astounded and said, 'Where did this man get this wisdom and these deeds of power? Is not this the carpenter's son? Is not his mother called Mary? And are not his brothers James and Joseph and Simon and Judas? And are not all his sisters with us? Where then did this man get all this?' And they took offense at him. But Jesus said to them, 'Prophets are not without honor except in their own country and in their own house.' And he did not do many deeds of power there, because of their unbelief" (Matthew 13:54-56).

There is a striking change in wisdom and in power when one realizes that one is loved totally and irrevocably. Karl Barth spoke of the freedom to trust that comes of this realization.

"Our human path is, as such, a path from one disloyalty to another; and it is the same with the ways of the gods of this world. They do not keep what they promise. So with them there is never any real peace and clarity. In God alone is there faithfulness, and faith is the trust that we may hold to Him, to His promise and to His guidance. To hold to God is to rely on the fact that God is there for me, and to live in this certainty. This is the promise that God gives us: I am there for you. . . . Because God is for us, we may also be for Him. Because He has given Himself to us, we may also in gratitude give Him the trifle which we have to give. To hold to God thus always means that we receive everything wholly from God and so are wholly active for Him" (*Church Dogmatics in Outline* [New York: Harper & Row, 1959], p. 19).

Jesus knew that His Father loved Him. That was the source of His authority. He could thus face with equanimity the interrogation of the demanding, hair-splitting chief priests and elders in the last week of His life on earth. He told them: "I'll answer your question if you answer mine: John's baptism, what was its origin, heavenly or human?" When you know, really know, that God loves you, then you do not fear the sick and the dead; you are not repulsed by the broken and the disfigured; you cannot be embarrassed by the shamed and the shaming. The authority of Jesus Christ to heal and to redeem is found in the love of His Father and ours, experienced in the Jordan, crossing from what was to what is and ever shall be. The apostle Paul said hardship, distress, persecution, famine, nakedness, danger, or violence can't strip that love away from us.

"For I am convinced that neither death, nor life, nor angels, nor rulers, nor things present, nor things to come, nor powers, nor height, nor depth, nor anything else in all creation, will be able to separate us from the love of God in Christ Jesus our Lord" (Romans 8:38, 39).

The sky closed overhead. The thunder faded. Jesus turned around as a man under the compulsion of love. John watched Him leave the river, not to the west bank, from where He had come, but to the east bank, where He hiked alone up out of the gorge and into the wilderness beyond. It was a place that John knew as few men did, a solitary place where the ache of loneliness and the desperation of emptiness could test whether a human could live without the safety of limits and the comfort of compromise. John noticed the Spirit light still shining on Jesus' back as if pushing Him up and out into the rocks and hard places.

When Jesus was gone, John turned back to the crowd waiting for him. "You know the One that I have been telling you about, the One who will baptize you with fire. Well, let me tell you what just happened and what it means for you."

You, child of the same Father, reading this in the rocks and hard places of your life, know that He is God and He loves you. You are at the crossing from alienation to full acceptance. "The river of God is full of water" (Psalm 65:9), and there is enough for you.

FORTY-ONE

Lord, Spend Me

Discovering that we are currency in the hand of God meant to be spent at His will and for His service.

Jesus "sat down opposite the [temple] treasury, and watched the crowd putting money into the treasury. Many rich people put in large sums. A poor widow came and put in two small copper coins, which are worth a penny. Then he called his disciples and said to them, 'Truly I tell you this poor widow has put in more than all those who are contributing to the treasury. For all of them have contributed out of their abundance; but she out of her poverty has put in everything she had, all she had to live on'" (Mark 12:41-44).

Contrast this story with this one told by Henri Nouwen:

An elderly woman was brought to a psychiatric center. "She was wild, swinging at everything in sight, and scaring everyone so much that the doctor had to take everything away from her. But there was one small coin which she gripped in her fist and would not give up. In fact, it took two people to pry open that squeezed hand. It was as though she would lose her very self along with the coin. If they deprived her of that last possession, she would have nothing more, and be nothing more. That was her fear" (Henri J. M. Nouwen, *With Open Hands* [New York: Ballantine Books, 1990], p. 3).

Between these stories lies the frontier of faith. If you think either story is about money, think again. Money is valuable only for what it can buy. If you are marooned at the South Pole with nothing more than $1 million in cash you are going to die. The coins of these women represented their life. The widow gave up "all she had to live on"—in essence, her life. The elderly psychiatric patient could not give up her life.

Think about what you can or can't live without. Think about what you are grasping, even hoarding. Is it your job? a relationship? a bank account?

image? influence? power? a secret thought of revenge? a dream? a cause?

Do you and I go through our days carefully guarding our turf, saving our strength, storing up for a pleasant retirement? Does our hope boil down to the description of T. S. Eliot, "the asphalt road and a thousand lost golf balls"?

"For what are you saving your life?" is a question that I am asking myself and others these days. We live comfortably and carefully. We go through the motions, not wanting to make waves. We tell each other "Don't be rash," mistaking rashness for the risk-taking inherent in the life of faith. Robert Wicks writes:

"Being rash is the result of thoughtless impulse. Risking is knowing that there are some things we must do—even when we feel they may involve making mistakes or even failure. The reality we must be willing to look at and accept is: being on the road to finding the truth or seeking improvement is, at best, a hazardous process. Still, it is one we cannot avoid if we wish to live a full spiritual life, even when the temptation to hold back seems so sensible" (Robert Wicks, *Seeds of Sensitivity* [Notre Dame, Ind.: Ave Maria Press, 1995], p. 70).

Jesus told a story about a wealthy ruler who needed to go on a long business trip. He placed his fortune in a blind trust with 10 of his subordinates, instructing them to use the capital to operate the enterprise until his return. On his return the ruler called in the first subordinate and asked how he did with the money. The subordinate said he'd invested it and made a 100 percent return on the principal" The ruler said that was great, and because he was trustworthy in this small job, he would make him the governor of 10 towns. The second subordinate reported that he had invested the principal entrusted to him and made a return of 50 percent. The ruler rewarded him with the governorship of five towns.

The next subordinate told a different story. "'Master, here's your money safe and sound. I kept it hidden in the cellar. To tell you the truth, I was a little afraid. I know you have high standards and hate sloppiness, and don't suffer fools gladly.'

"He said, 'You're right that I don't suffer fools gladly—and you've acted the fool! Why didn't you at least invest the money in securities so I would have gotten a little interest on it?'

"Then he said to those standing there, 'Take the money from him and give it to the servant who doubled my stake.'

"They said, 'But Master, he already has double . . . '

"He said, 'That's what I mean: Risk your life and get more than you ever dreamed of. Play it safe and end up holding the bag'" (Luke 19:20-26, Message).

This is a story of grace. If all is God's, then why play it safe? Handkerchiefs are meant to clean up messes, bind wounds, wipe runny noses, and mop sweaty brows. These are all byproducts of action. The passive use of the handkerchief as a wallet is exhibit A that no risk was taken. If God can obtain an investment, then He operates in grace—His power, not our effort. He expects us to use what we are given and not stand pat in cringing paralysis that if we lose what we have, there won't be more.

But again, these aren't stories about money and stuff. Jesus did not come to establish endowments and build portfolios. He said, "I came that they may have life, and have it abundantly" (John 10:10). You can read the Gospels through and through and you will never find anything that says Jesus wants us to be conservative with our lives. Obedient, moral, ethical, yes—but not conservative and self-protective. He also said: "Whoever wishes to become great among you must be your servant, and whoever wishes to be first among you must be slave of all. For the Son of Man came not to be served but to serve, and to give his life a ransom for many" (Mark 10:43, 44).

Jesus' valuation of His life and the life that He gives you and me is that it is a ransom. A ransom is something worth exchanging. We are the currency of God. We are His to spend and His to invest. Why, indeed, are we trying to save our own lives? We were not meant to be banked and held in reserve. We are meant to be spent by God.

Dag Hammarskjold wrote this in his journal in 1957: "You will know Life and be acknowledged by it according to your degree of transparency, your capacity, that is, to vanish as an end, and remain purely as a means." "'The best and most wonderful thing that can happen to you in this life, is that you should be silent and let God work and speak.' Long ago, you gripped me, Slinger. *Now* into the storm. *Now* towards your target" (*Markings* [New York: Alfred A. Knopf, 1964], p. 156).

When I came to this understanding that I am currency in the hand of God, I was so overwhelmed that I wrote a song about it. I played and sang it only once for two friends, and their reaction was that the lyrics terrified them. They felt so strongly about it that I never brought it out again, but I often sing and pray these words when I am alone. They express the understanding of my heart about God's will.

> As water in a thirsty desert,
> As coins in a beggar's hand,
> As a candle in the darkness,
> As salt poured on the bland,
> Lord spend me.
>
> Spend me lavishly,
> Use me recklessly,
> To love extravagantly,
> Lord spend me.
>
> As fresh bread for the hungry,
> As vision for the blind,
> Whatever, Lord, Your purpose,
> Take my body, soul, and mind,
> And spend me.
>
> Spend me lavishly,
> Use me recklessly,
> To love extravagantly,
> Lord, spend me.

—Copyright © 1994 by Kent A. Hansen

Abba: Take us. We plunge into the stream of Your grace. No holding back. Spend us where and as You will. Yes!

FORTY-TWO

Facing the Wind

The invitation of Jesus is a call to face the wind.

Our house is being lashed by wind and rain on the afternoon that I write this. A surprising spring storm has blown off the Pacific. I love it!

According to Hansen family lore, the day that my parents brought me home from the hospital after birth I turned my face toward the open car window, opened my mouth, and drank in the breeze. It must be true, for I can never resist the power of a wind. On our honeymoon Patricia and I stood on grassy hills above Big Sur at sunset, spreading our jackets wide and letting the gale howling off the open ocean lift and blow us backward up the hill. One of the greatest hikes I've ever made was in 40-mile-per-hour winter winds along the bluffs above the Monterey Bay with my 5-month-old son asleep, snug and secure in a pack against my chest inside my parka. Earlier this year I called Patricia at 1:30 a.m. from the twenty-second floor of a hotel in San Antonio to share with her the roar of an approaching Texas thunderstorm. I couldn't sleep for the sheer joy of the wind and the lightning.

There are gaps high in the San Gabriel Mountains where I like to stand on the border between the high desert to the east and the ocean plain to the west. The wind shrieks through these gaps in the rush of pressure changes between the two climate zones. My favorite place of prayer is the trunk of a giant gnarled cedar that clings to the cliff edge beside one of these natural wind tunnels.

There is an expression of God in the wind. David recognized this. "The voice of the Lord breaks the cedars. . . . The voice of the Lord causes the oaks to whirl, and strips the forest bare; and in his temple all say, 'Glory'" (Psalm 29:5-9). When the Holy Spirit manifested itself to the New Testament believers at Pentecost it arrived from heaven "like the rush of a violent wind, and it filled the entire house where they were sitting" (Acts 2:2).

Like its Creator, the wind breaks what resists it. Caught in the open with nowhere to hide, one can confront the wind and be snapped in pieces, or run with the wind and live. That is the choice Paul described: "A violent wind, called the northeaster, rushed down from Crete. Since the ship was caught and could not be turned head-on into the wind, we gave way to it and were driven" (Acts 27:14, 15). Those who wish to live beyond the storm become one with it, riding the power of the wind. Those who would live beyond the storm front between God and their own wills must become at one with God, riding the Spirit's power.

Thus it is that I take encouragement from the story of John Muir, the great naturalist and Christian believer, who sought to be one with the storm. Here is Muir's story as told by Eugene Peterson:

"In 1874, Muir visited a friend who had a cabin, snug in a valley of the Yuba River in the Sierra Mountains—a place from which to venture into the wilderness and then return for a comforting cup of tea.

"One December day a storm moved in from the Pacific—a fierce storm that bent the junipers and the pines, the madronas and fir trees as if they were so many blades of grass. It was for just such times this cabin had been built: cozy protection from the harsh elements. We easily imagine Muir and his host safe and secure in his tightly caulked cabin, a fire blazing against the cruel assault of the elements, wrapped in sheep skins, Muir meditatively rendering the wildness into his elegant prose. But our imaginations, not trained to cope with Muir, betray us. For Muir, instead of retreating to the coziness of the cabin, pulling the door tight, and throwing another stick of wood on the fire, strode *out* of the cabin into the storm, climbed a high ridge, picked a giant Douglas fir as the best perch for experiencing the kaleidoscope of color and the sound, scent and motion, scrambled his way to the top, and rode out the storm, lashed by the wind, holding on for dear life, relishing weather: taking it all in—its rich sensuality, its primal energy" (foreword to Luci Shaw, *Water My Soul* [Grand Rapids: Zondervan, 1998], pp. 9, 10, retelling Edwin Way Teale, ed., *The Wilderness World of John Muir* [Boston: Houghton-Mifflin, 1954], pp. 181-190).

It is a treasured myth of the religious life that its goal is to find a safe haven, sheltered from the wind, and stand pat there. It is a myth because the world turns and we grow. To seek shelter and hide there is not to live. God's call is a call to movement. The strength and peace that we are promised is a peace of heart in our inner being, where Christ dwells through our faith like my infant son bundled warm and secure against my chest inside my coat as I walked through the winter gale. To avoid the wind is to give up on life as it was meant to be lived.

It was the wind (breath/spirit) of God that swept the earth and brought life and light from chaos and darkness at Creation (Genesis 1:2). It is the wind of the Spirit that created the life of Jesus (Luke 1:35). The wind of God's Spirit holds the key to new and lasting life for all living things, even you and me. "When you send your Spirit, they are created, and you renew the face of the earth" (Psalm 104:30, NIV). Jesus spoke this truth to Nicodemus:

"Very truly, I tell you, no one can enter the kingdom of God without being born of water and Spirit. What is born of the flesh is flesh, and what is born of the Spirit is spirit. Do not be astonished that I said to you, 'You must be born from above.' The wind blows where it chooses, and you hear the sound of it, but you do not know where it comes from or where it goes. So it is with everyone who is born of the Spirit" (John 3:5-8).

Are you hiding from the wind, hanging on against its power, obsessed with safety? Do you realize the futility of this effort?

"For every matter has its time and way, although the troubles of mortals lie heavy upon them. Indeed, they do not know what is to be, for who can tell them how it will be? No one has power over the wind to restrain the wind, or power over the day of death; there is no discharge from the battle" (Ecclesiastes 8:6-8).

Jesus, the only one whom the wind and waves obey, calls you to cross the sea with Him, to ride the wind through the dark to the other side (Luke 8:22, 23). "Where is your faith?" He asks (verse 25). Your God, your help, comes for you "swiftly upon the wings of the wind" (Psalm 18:10). So turn from your fear and clenched handholds, run with the wind, and live free in Christ.

FORTY-THREE

Strawberry Pop Grace

A thirsty young couple find a delightful blessing in a sand dune.

My girlfriend Sylvia and I walked down the shore of the Monterey Bay one afternoon. We were college students home for vacation. Our goal was the estuary of the Pajaro River.

Even with the temperate ocean breezes, the sun reflecting off white sand and water and the coastal humidity made us hot and sticky.

We had brought no water with us. Our conversation turned to what we would like to drink right there and then. We considered and discarded different options. Then Sylvia said, "What I'd really like is an ice-cold strawberry soda."

"That would be great," I agreed. "I can taste it now."

We were ascending a sand dune, and right in our path we spied a can of strawberry soda. We laughed, and I picked it up. The can was full and intact, though warm. We could have placed it in the surf to cool it down somewhat before drinking it. But overwhelmed by our serendipitous discovery, we chose instead to keep the can as a memento of a fun day. We endured our dry throats the rest of the hike.

Grace is like this. We long and thirst in a time of drought. Then the rains come, maybe even a torrent, and we can't decide whether to catch it in buckets, stand with our mouths open drinking it in, sandbag the front yard against floods, or take a swim.

Three of David's closest companions in his campaign to rout the Philistines out of the Valley of Rephaim overheard David say longingly, "'O that someone would give me water to drink from the well of Bethlehem that is by the gate!' Then the Three broke through the camp of the Philistines, and drew water from the well of Bethlehem that was by the gate, and they brought it to David. But David would not drink of it; he poured it out to the Lord, and said, 'My God forbid that I should do this.

Can I drink the blood of these men? For at the risk of their lives they brought it.' Therefore he would not drink it" (1 Chronicles 11:17-19).

Simon Peter fished all night and caught nothing. Then Jesus told him to throw his net in the water one more time. Peter said, " 'Master, we've been fishing hard all night and haven't caught even a minnow. But if you say so, I'll let out the nets.' It was no sooner said than done—a huge haul of fish, straining the nets past capacity. They waved to their partners in the other boat to come help them. They filled both boats, nearly swamping them with the catch.

"Simon Peter, when he saw it, fell to his knees before Jesus. 'Master, leave. I'm a sinner and I can't handle this holiness. Leave me to myself' " (Luke 5:5-8, Message).

The reactions of David and Peter are authentic. We have all witnessed or expressed protestations of unworthiness at great and costly gifts or displays of kindness. Much rarer, however, is the reaction of a grateful thank-you. There is only one thank-you to Jesus said in the entire Gospel record. On His final journey to Jerusalem and the cross, Jesus encountered a group of 10 lepers begging Him for mercy. He sent them to the priests for confirmation of their healing, and on the way they were healed and cleansed of the loathsome, disfiguring rot that had made them outcasts. Only one of them returned to thank Jesus. Before the healing, he was a triple outcast, being of mixed race, a member of a despised religious minority, and a public health menace. Jesus marveled at the precious singularity of the thank-you coming from a foreigner and the lack of expression of gratitude from the Jews (Luke 17:11-19).

Why are we more likely to respond to grace with an "I'm unworthy, Lord" than a simple "thank-You"? Because it is hard for us to believe that it isn't all about us—that everything depends on whether we are deserving or undeserving because of our intentions and actions. One thing a young lawyer learns quickly is the ingratitude of clients. If the judgment is favorable, the client often thinks it is because he or she was right all along and had such a good case that the lawyer wasn't necessary after all. If the case is lost, many clients are quick to blame their lawyer. Are we any different about the way we treat God over the way things turn out for us?

To say thank you is to acknowledge that it is not about us and that there is another source outside of us on which we are dependent. That acknowledgment cuts to the core of our proud, sinful, rebellious hearts. It is our clever dodge of this unmasking of our vulnerability to say, "Well, you know that I'm grateful by the way I act." But how many hearts are withered waiting for the words "Thank you," or "I love you." To say thank you is to recognize that we have received from another; that we are not complete in ourselves. Gratitude is the umbilical cord of grace, and "thank you" is the password of the humble. Brennan Manning describes this phenomena:

"Underlying every cry of the grateful sinner is an unshaken trust in the person and promise of Jesus. Jesus' parables of the sheer gratuity of grace rustle like refreshing rain on the parched ground of pharisaical piety, sweep like a wild storm into the glum corners of sentimental hallelujah religion, and vibrate like sharp lightning in the sulfurous atmosphere of legalists hell-bent on nonhistorical orthodoxy" (*Ruthless Trust* [San Francisco: Harper, 2000], p. 29).

A can of strawberry pop found in a sand dune cannot be reasonably compared to the sacrifice of love and life that brought David his drink or the miracle of Jesus' love that brought Peter to his knees in confession or the leper prostrate at Jesus' feet. But grace is to be taken where it is found. Perhaps you will find grace in the hug of a loved one, a long-distance call, the laughter of a child, the contentment of a family gathered, a prayer answered, a meal lovingly prepared, forgiveness extended, and reconciliation achieved. Who knows what you may find if you look? Something both as ordinary and as wonderful as a can of strawberry soda in a sand dune.

David pondered such blessings and wrote:

> What can I give back to God
>   for the blessings he's poured out on me?
> I'll lift high the cup of salvation—a toast to God;
>   I'll pray in the name of God!
> I'll complete what I promised God I'd do,
>   and I'll do it together with his people (Psalm 116:12-14,
>   Message).

Look for grace, desire it, and receive it with the simple but always appropriate word "Thanks."

FORTY-FOUR

God Forgives Us

The heart of grace is God's forgiveness of us.

All the elements were there that Friday—all the things that large and small, catastrophic and merely inconvenient, excruciating and uncomfortable make this life anywhere from difficult to unbearable. There was abrasion and laceration, blood and grit, riven flesh, curses, misunderstanding, hatred, lies, rough splinters against smooth skin, cowardice, ignorance, malevolence, and the sticky spit of uncouth mockers. All of this was arrayed against one person under a merciless desert sun. That person entered the world as a diapered infant, apprenticed as a carpenter, and spoke of the meaning of existence in a fresh and direct manner. He so devalued the religious and societal status quo that those who profited by it killed Him as a cost of doing business.

Why? What is worth dying for? Doesn't it make a lot of sense to go along to get along?

I ask a different question: What business of ours is worth protecting to the point of killing the Son of God?

Security—our security—seems to us to justify killing the Son of God. We want to be secure. Our automobiles are made sleeker and more powerful with less bulk to aid in gas mileage. Speed kills. Collisions at 75 mph with bridge abutments or with other cars moving at similar speed kill people. We don't want to die, but we don't want to slow down. So we wrap ourselves in seat belts, install air bags, and sue somebody when these devices don't work.

It used to be that our children were taught in kindergarten to be polite to adults. Now they are taught that if an adult speaks to them they should call the police. We can move our money electronically around the world in seconds, but fear to approach the automatic teller machine after dark. Communism falls, the nuclear threat diminishes, but the World

Trade Center vaporizes, land mines are strewn in Kosovo, and 800,000 people, many of them baptized Christians, are hacked to death with machetes, many wielded by baptized Christians, in Rwanda.

We fear death. We are unwilling to turn off ventilators for loved ones with flat brain waves in intensive-care units. There are an estimated 70 million registered guns in the state of Texas alone. There are bars on our windows, alarms on our cars, mace in our pockets, and panic in our hearts.

Thousands of years ago a question was put: "Did God tell you that if you eat of the tree of the knowledge of good and evil, you will surely die?" An answer was given and accepted: "Surely you will not die." And we have been dying ever since, and it infuriates us.

Why can't we figure it out? Why can't we live forever? It isn't fair! With our knowledge of good and evil we build machines, transplant organs, take drugs, and worship youth to defeat death. In our quest for the ultimate security we build strongholds for protection and attack each other as "security threats."

Jesus was killed as a security threat. He healed people without cost, He forgave their sins, He spoke to them in language they could understand, and He raised His friend Lazarus from the dead. His grace was both the illustration of human delusions of competence and the antidote to human brokenness. It was too much for the leaders and the theologians. Their chief said, "You guys don't get the threat that Jesus really is. If we let Him go on like this, our monopoly on holiness is broken. It is better that He die and we keep the franchise on goodness." From that day they planned His death (John 11:45-53).

However, in the words of Joseph, "You meant evil against me; but God meant it for good" (Genesis 50:20, NKJV). If the Creator turns His life over to the created to do with as they will, there is no doubting His love for His creatures. And being the Creator, He can give His life to His creatures. "For this reason the Father loves me, because I lay down my life in order to take it up again. No one takes it from me, but I lay it down of my own accord. I have power to lay it down, and I have power to take it up again" (John 10:17, 18). In the same passage Jesus speaks of us: "I came that they may have life, and have it abundantly" (verse 10). Curiously, in the Old Testament a life for a life was an act of vengeance. In the New Testament a life for a life is forgiveness. This is the essence of grace. No one took the life of Jesus; He gave it as a complete atoning sacrifice for sin, God with us even in death, doing what we cannot do so that we can be with God forever in life. This is the forgiveness of God. It is the ultimate forgiveness, the strong taking the place of the weak, the Divine standing in as humanity for humanity.

The first Christian school in which we enrolled our son had a curious project in the second grade. The students were asked to bring large fruit or coffee cans that they decorated with paper wrapping and religious symbols. Then they were sent home with the instruction to the parents that each time the child did something right or obeyed, we parents were to place a coin in the can. Then the child was to bring it back to school as a fund-raiser. This was met with resistance, even derision, in our home. The idea of material reward for obedience is far removed from our theology. We are raising a human being, not Pavlov's dog. My brother Terry came up with the winning solution: Fill the can with coins and send it back with Andrew the very next day along with a note that says, "Andrew is under grace, not the law."

Paul wrote, of the simple motivation of Christ: "For freedom Christ has set us free. Stand firm, therefore, and do not submit again to a yoke of slavery" (Galatians 5:1). Slavery is self-protection, watching out for what the other person might do to us. Slavery is violence, protecting what is ours and revenging our insults. Slavery is toil and stress, competing for finite resources without reliance on the providence of an infinite Creator. Slavery is slander, putting down others so we stand higher. Slavery is resentment, locking ourselves to those who have wounded or betrayed us while we replay the videotape over and over. Slavery is unforgiveness.

Freedom is God doing what we can't do for ourselves. One of my favorite definitions of Christianity is this: "In every other religion, it is what you do; with Christ it is done." Imagine a future with God where we don't have to work and scrape to survive, where pain and tears are unknown, where strategic alliances for protection and defense are unnecessary, where the guardedness of our daily existence is obsolete, where sermons telling others how to live will be meaningless. Forgiveness, not having anyone threatening to destroy us, is freedom. Do we trust our forgiveness? Or do we cave to our fears and live badly?

When I was growing up, we would gather in the living room for family worship. Sometimes we would say our favorite Scripture passage to each other. With my dad it was always this: "For God so loved the world that He gave His only begotten Son, that whoever believes in Him should not perish but have everlasting life" (John 3:16, NKJV). A forgiven life is a new life is a free life. Here is a description of that life from Paul, written in contemporary language:

"Our firm decision is to work from this focused center: One man died for everyone. That puts everyone in the same boat. He included everyone in his death so that everyone could also be included in his life, a resurrection life, a far better life than people ever lived on their own.

"Because of this decision we don't evaluate people by what they have or how they look. We looked at the Messiah that way once and got it all wrong, as you know. We certainly don't look at Him that way anymore. Now we look inside, and what we see is that anyone united with the Messiah gets a fresh start, is created new. The old life is gone; a new life burgeons. Look at it! All this comes from the God who settled the relationship between us and Him, and then called us to settle our relationships with each other. God put the world square with Himself through the Messiah, giving the world a fresh start by offering forgiveness of sins. God has given us the task of telling everyone what He is doing. We're Christ's representatives. God uses us to persuade men and women to drop their differences and enter into God's work of making things right between them. We're speaking for Christ Himself now: Become friends with God; He's already a friend with you.

"How? you ask. In Christ. God put the wrong on Him who never did anything wrong so we could be put right with God" (see 2 Corinthians 5:16-21, Message).

Child of grace, you are forgiven by your God. Live like it. Live large and free.

FORTY-FIVE

Family Worship

*Aging father and middle-aged son share the gift of music
and hope in a precious moment of family worship.*

I visited my parents at their home in rural northern California in March 2001. The next time I saw them my dad was in the hospital with an illness that led to successful open heart surgery. Since then they have moved to our town to live closer to us. After the March visit I wrote an entry in my journal that I want to share with you.

"Would you like to take a nap?" my mom asks her middle-aged son.

"No, I don't like to sleep during the day."

"Neither do I," says Dad.

"I never sleep during the day," I say, "unless I'm in a committee meeting. Then I do it only for anesthetic purposes."

Dad laughs.

I reach down in my briefcase, past the work in progress and the work to be started, and pull out my harmonica. I blow a note or two.

"Oh, you brought your harmonica," Dad says. "I was hoping that you would."

He disappears into the bedroom and comes out with the Hohner Goliath harmonica that I bought him many years ago. He sits down in his rocker opposite from me and we begin to play. This is soft and easy music made by two men who could follow its melodic paths in the dark.

"Man," Dad says to me, "you know songs that I'd forgotten all about."

"I love the old hymns."

"So do I, and the new hymnals don't have the great old songs."

We play on.

Dad's bald head glows bronze in the afternoon light of a warm March

Monday. His big gnarled hands grasp the harmonica and move it across his lips like corn on the cob. Through the screen door I see a doe and yearling cropping spring grass under the oaks. The Rhodesian Ridgeback dog from across the road kept the deer away for years. A month ago she was paralyzed by tick-borne Lyme's disease. Dad fed her after her owner died of cancer, leaving the place abandoned and the dog orphaned. When the county veterinarian came to put her down, Dad watched unflinchingly, talking softly to the dog, scratching her ears until she stopped breathing.

I blow the four-note ascent beginning "Londonderry Air."

"We're going to make Mama cry," Dad said.

We stop and replenish her Kleenex. Then we play on while she bawls and we grin and shrug. She always cries during that song. We'd be disappointed if she didn't.

On and on we play, thinking of songs, drinking cold sweet water from deep in the well of our life together. These songs explain our God to us, define our faith, stretch our hearts, remind us of God's love in the dark times. We share the gift of music like a loaf of fresh bread between two hungry friends. The notes flow through us and around us to burnish our memories and our hopes to a warm patina.

The piano and organ that once stood side by side in my parents' living room are gone. The piano is at my home, where my son learns these songs. The organ has gone to a friend who plays it with the tender touch that my folks always insisted upon when it was played by one of us. Life has its way of returning us to the fundamentals, and a 91-year-old father and a 47-year-old son playing hymns together on mouth organs is about as fundamental as it gets.

One of us leads, the other follows, the order dictated only by the one of us who remembers first. Somewhere the secretaries in two offices are taking my phone messages and explaining my absence. It is Monday, after all. Work beckons from the briefcase at my feet, but there is a transcendent power in worship that picks us up and sets us down in secret and holy places accessed by grace alone.

We forget the melody sometimes and start over unashamed. We wander off into other tunes. We soar and hush, and finally fade away.

Then Dad asks what he always asks at the end of these sessions. "Do you know this one?" He plays and I follow into a familiar song of our

fondest hope. The words are held in our souls, the melody brings them up
to our minds.

My heart can sing when I pause to remember
A heartache here is but a stepping stone
Along a trail that's winding always upward,
This troubled world is not my final home.

The things of earth will dim and lose their value
If we recall they're borrowed for awhile;
And things of earth that cause the heart to tremble,
Remembered there will only bring a smile.

But until then my heart will go on singing,
Until then with joy I'll carry on
Until the day my eyes behold the city,
Until the day God calls me home.

—Stuart Hamblen, Copyright
1958, Hamblen Music Co., Inc.